D1591018

DISCARDED

*The Mediterranean Strategy in the Second World War*

# The Mediterranean Strategy
# in the Second World War

___

THE LEES–KNOWLES LECTURES AT
TRINITY COLLEGE, CAMBRIDGE
1966

___

## MICHAEL E. HOWARD

WEIDENFELD AND NICOLSON
5 Winsley Street London W1

Printed in Great Britain
by Ebenezer Baylis & Son Limited
The Trinity Press, Worcester, and London

*This study is dedicated to the
Master and Fellows of Trinity College,
Cambridge, at whose invitation the
original lectures were delivered
in autumn 1966*

# Contents

# Foreword

ALTHOUGH the debate over the effectiveness of Allied strategy in the Second World War began, among those who were party to its making, long before the war itself had ended, it was some five years before it became a matter of general public concern. By then the high hopes of 1945, that the sacrifices of the United Nations would produce a new world peacefully united under the Rule of Law, had sadly faded. The United States, the British Commonwealth and their allies in Western Europe found themselves confronted by a hostile power whose totalitarian methods and ideological ambitions appeared to menace their own security no less than had those of the Third Reich. Misunderstanding and mutual suspicion rapidly created a state of international tension which by 1950 seemed quite likely to lead to yet a third world war. In such an atmosphere a search for scapegoats was natural enough. As the Second World War itself had been attributed to the mistakes of the statesmen responsible for French and British policy in the 1930s, so the makers of Allied strategy in the 1940s were now blamed for having failed to foresee the probable shape of the post-war world and devise their plans accordingly.

Pre-eminent among the writers who opened the debate were two great military journalists: Hanson Baldwin, the title of whose work *Great Mistakes of the War* (1950) speaks for itself; and Chester Wilmot, whose brilliant study *The Struggle for Europe* (1952) not only established the first full narrative of Allied strategic planning and operations, but

pronounced judgements which are still widely held to be
authoritative. The picture which emerged from these and
lesser works was one of a subtle, far-sighted and politically
motivated British strategy, devised primarily by Winston
Churchill, which would, but for American short-sightedness
and doctrinaire stupidity, not only have won the war with a
minimum of bloodshed, but have placed the West in an
advantageous position *vis-à-vis* the Soviet Union after it.
Wilmot himself admitted that he regarded

The Second Front controversy . . . not merely in the light of its
influence on the defeat of Germany, but also as a political issue
the outcome of which was that Anglo-American military power
was employed in Western Europe, not in the Balkans. . . . In the
summer of 1944 the Western Allies had it in their power, if not to
end the war against Germany that year, at least to ensure that the
great capitals of Central Europe – Berlin, Prague and Vienna –
would be liberated from Nazi rule by the West, not the East.[1]

This view found ready acceptance, not only among British
readers inclined to attribute their misfortunes to the mis-
calculations of their allies, but among Americans equally
willing to blame them on President Roosevelt. Neither group
was numerically inconsiderable. Although Churchill himself
never made such explicit claims, evidence to substantiate them
could easily be quarried from the six volumes of his own
*The Second World War* which appeared between 1948 and 1954;
especially since these, being based on his own minutes and
memoranda rather than on the papers of the Chiefs of Staff
and their sub-committees, gave only a partial account of the
process by which British strategy was formulated and carried
out. But the most powerful reinforcement for this argument
was to come with the publication, in 1957 and 1959, of Sir
Arthur Bryant's two volumes based on Lord Alanbrooke's

[1] Chester Wilmot, *The Struggle for Europe* (London 1952), p. 12–13.

papers – *The Turn of the Tide* and *Triumph in the West*. These, while attributing the authorship of British strategy almost solely to Lord Alanbrooke, gave passionate endorsement to Wilmot's judgement; more passionate, in the view of some critics, even than Lord Alanbrooke's own observations warranted.

Sir Arthur Bryant's first volume provoked an equally powerful and nationalistic response from the other side of the Atlantic in Professor S. E. Morison's *American Contributions to the Strategy of World War II*.[1] But by this time a great deal more evidence had become available with the publication of British and American official histories and memoirs. The fears and political passions which had done so much to provoke the controversy in the first place were dying down, and a more balanced picture was emerging. By 1963 it was possible for an American scholar, Dr Richard M. Leighton, to write:

We now know . . . that responsible British leaders never advocated an Allied invasion of the Balkan peninsula and that the 'Balkans versus Western Europe' controversy referred to by many post-war writers is a myth. . . . The familiar stereotype that pictures the British as persistently manœuvring at the conference table and behind the scenes to weaken and postpone the cross-channel invasion, while striving to build up the Mediterranean Theatre at its expense . . . is not consistent with the findings of post-war research.[2]

The controversy which Wilmot provoked and to which Leighton refers centred around the conflicting claims of OVERLORD, the Allied invasion of North-West Europe, and

---

[1] London, Oxford University Press, 1958.

[2] Richard M. Leighton, 'Overlord Revisited', *The American Historical Review*, July 1963. Mr John Ehrman had already given an authoritative account of Mr Churchill's attitude to the Balkans in Appendix VI to his volume in the U.K. Official Histories of the Second World War, *Grand Strategy*, vol. V (London 1956).

the 'Mediterranean strategy' advocated by the British Chiefs of Staff. It is not my purpose to pronounce any new judgements on a controversy which is, as Leighton rightly says, no longer a live issue among scholars. But among a wider public many of the misconceptions to which Wilmot gave currency still enjoy considerable circulation. The essay which follows is simply an attempt to establish what this 'Mediterranean strategy' actually was: how it originated, how it developed, and what its authors hoped to achieve by it. Whether or not it was 'correct', and whether divergence from it was a 'mistake', I shall leave it to historians bolder than myself to judge.

# I

# *The Shaping of British Strategy,*
# *1939-41*

IT has sometimes been suggested that the makers of British strategy in the Second World War were guided by a traditional wisdom derived from three centuries' experience of making war against a continental adversary: experience which the Americans did not share and to which they should have deferred. Mr Wilmot and Sir Arthur Bryant made this point in almost identical terms:

> The British [wrote Chester Wilmot] . . . have never been numerically strong enough in war to proceed on the basis of riding rough-shod over the enemy. They have had to win their campaigns by manœuvre, not by mass . . . They knew from long experience of European wars that would-be invaders must first exploit the great mobility which sea-power (and now air-power) gave them, in order to keep the enemy dispersed and to counter his natural advantage of being able to move on interior lines.[1]

Sir Arthur Bryant described British strategy as being based on

the history of a sea-based Army which always had to fight with inadequate resources and which, through many costly failures, had learned to offset that handicap by using sea power to hold the enemy with the minimum of force along the widest possible

[1] Wilmot, op. cit., p. 129.

circumference while concentrating striking-strength at the point where it could be most effectively used.[1]

This thesis is open to question on at least three counts. The first is the extent to which historical precedent either consciously or unconsciously inspired British strategic thought during the Second World War. The second is its accuracy as a description of what sea-power had actually achieved in Britain's earlier wars. And the third is the relevance of precedents drawn from the age of sail to the conditions of war in the mid-twentieth century.

Any historian who has enjoyed access to the papers of the Chiefs of Staff is likely to have doubts about the first of these questions. It is quite true that the Prime Minister drew deep on his vast knowledge of historical precedent in composing the eloquent and erudite memoranda which he pressed on his military advisers. It is not so clear that those which depended most on historical arguments were those which the Chiefs of Staff found most convincing, or which usually carried the day. The development of British – and Allied – strategy was a piecemeal affair, in which the military leaders had often simply to do what they could, where they could, with the forces which they had to hand. Historical precedent can sometimes be illuminating, sometimes inspiring, but often it can be misleading as well. All too often, military and naval history is itself written to prove theses which a more scholarly examination of the evidence does not bear out; and one cannot help wondering upon which historians Mr Wilmot and Sir Arthur Bryant were basing themselves when they drew these sweeping conclusions about the lessons which could be learned, and which they alleged *had* been learned, from Britain's military past.

Had it in fact ever been possible to use sea-power as they

---

[1] Arthur Bryant, *Triumph in the West* (London 1959), p. 33.

described, to enforce dispersal on the enemy and concentrate striking-strength at the most effective point? It had, but only on one condition: that Britain had powerful continental allies which could engage the bulk of the enemy's land forces. Then sea-power could be used, not only to effect useful diversions, but to bring those allies direct help. It could be used to enfeeble the economy of the enemy and recruit that of the allies. It made it possible for continental armies to win decisive victories, or, in the absence of such victories, to negotiate acceptable peace terms. But when these allies were either neutralized by enemy diplomacy or defeated in battle, British sea-power could achieve only very limited results. It could still preserve the British Isles and British trade intact. It could restrict the enemy's economy and harass his coasts. In days when wars were settled by gentlemanly negotiation it could make possible quite respectable peace terms – as indeed it might still have done in 1940, had Britain been inclined to make peace. But with all the advantages it gave in terms of manœuvre and flexibility, sea-power could not produce of itself a clear military decision; certainly not one of the kind for which Britain was fighting in the Second World War.

Even in eighteenth-century and Napoleonic warfare sea-power could give the British army, when it was fighting on the continent of Europe, only a limited degree of flexibility. Unless there was already a fighting ally to support, such as the British sometimes found in the Iberian Peninsula or in the Low Countries, amphibious landings could be as sterile and wasteful as was that at Walcheren in 1809. When with the coming of railways armies could move more swiftly by land than by sea, this flexibility was reduced still further. It was the harsh arguments of logistics which made British military planners, in the years before 1914, abandon the so-called 'British Way of Warfare' and concentrate their forces with those of their allies on the main battlefield. And to these were added, in the Second World War, the yet harsher arguments of land-based air-power, which made a mockery of the 'amphibious flexibility' of the British landings in Norway and Greece. The advantages of sea-power could now be exploited only by gathering a huge and highly vulnerable armada of transports, warships, aircraft carriers and their escorts and of specialized landing craft, whose target and operations had usually to be determined long in advance, whose assembly and movements were difficult to conceal, and whose call on allied resources was so great that alternative operations were virtually ruled out. Faced with this ponderous mode of attack it was the defender, moving up his reserves by road and rail, who enjoyed the flexibility; and it was the new weapon of air-power, rather than the traditional one of sea-power, that had to be called upon to counter it. These were the problems which the Chiefs of Staff faced in devising a strategy for attacking Hitler's *Festung Europa* between 1940 and 1944; and there is little evidence that historical precedents provided much help in solving them.

\*　　　\*　　　\*

Ever since the days of Napoleon it had been assumed by the strategists of Continental Europe – of the Powers, that is, among whom Britain had to find her allies – that the object in war was to force a decision by arms, and that this decision should be sought in major battle. Strategy therefore fell into three phases. First there was the mobilization of all available resources; not merely military preparations in peacetime but the acquisition of allies and of access to necessary economic resources – and, where possible, the denial of both to the enemy. Secondly there was the strategic deployment of forces, so that they could be used to the greatest possible advantage; combined with the simultaneous restriction of the strategic mobility of the enemy and the erosion of his strength. Finally there was the decisive engagement. If the first two phases had been carried out successfully – if an overwhelming preponderance of force had been mobilized and deployed in positions of equally overwhelming strategic advantage – the outcome of the decisive engagement might be so evident in advance to both sides that it did not take place at all; but it was always present to the minds of both adversaries – 'what cash payment is in bill transactions', to use Clausewitz's phrase[1] – and towards that engagement all planning was directed.

These concepts had dominated European military thought between 1870 and 1914, when rapid mobilization of the maximum resources to force an immediate decision had been the object of military planners in all the Great Powers of Europe. The decision in 1914–18, however, proved to be, not immediate, but prolonged and agonizing. There remained considerable doubt as to how far the great battles in the West had really been decisive at all. In any case the mobilization of manpower and material had dug so deeply into the resources of all the belligerents that none of them, victors or vanquished, were ever entirely to recover. There was therefore on all sides, in the years following 1918, a universal determination that war, if it were ever to recur, must avoid such a deadlock again. When, in March 1939, the British and French General Staffs began to discuss the shape of a war with Germany, they laid all their emphasis on the first of these three phases. Victory, they considered, must ultimately come as it had in the First World War, through the mobilization of superior resources of men and *matériel*. '*Nous gagnerons*', the French public and their allies were informed by large,

---

[1] Karl Maria von Clausewitz, *On War*, trans. J. J. Graham, ed. F. N. Maude (London 1962), vol. I, p. 40.

singularly uninspiring posters, '*parceque nous sommes les plus forts.*' German resources would be eroded by the blockade imposed by the superior Allied navies and by strategic bombardment from the air. Allied diplomacy in the Balkans and the Western Hemisphere would isolate Germany from possible friends and sources of supply. Ultimately, when a satisfactory superiority of *matériel* had been built up, the Allies would take the offensive; but to the form which that offensive would take, little thought had been given. In the circumstances of 1939, with Britain and France both trying desperately to make up the arrears of their armaments programmes and create the forces necessary for their mere defence, any such planning would have been grossly unrealistic. The ultimate strategic objective could thus be no more than a declaration of intent.

The intent could not be fulfilled, because the Germans struck before the Allies were ready and achieved victory by means hardly seen in Western Europe since the days of the young Bonaparte – the skilful strategic deployment of *inferior* strength. Strategic deployment, the second stage in continental warfare, had been almost lost to sight in Western Europe since the collapse of the grandiose Schlieffen Plan in 1914. *Tout le monde à la bataille!*, the massive accumulation of superior strength, had been the guiding principle of French and British strategy on the Western front. But in the German Army, which had continued to exploit such methods successfully on their Eastern Front throughout the First World War, the traditional expertise remained, and provided a solid foundation for the techniques of armoured warfare which they later learned from the pioneer British thinkers, J.F.C. Fuller and B.H. Liddell Hart. By such methods, they showed in May and June of 1940, they could again produce results as rapid and decisive as those achieved by the great masters of continental warfare, Napoleon and Helmuth von Moltke.

The following year the same techniques were used with equal success. The campaign in the Balkans in March and in Russia from June to December only confirmed that the Germans had succeeded in producing an engine of war which outclassed even their own formidable precedents.

What, in such a situation, were the British to do? The only instrument capable of bringing them decisive victory in classic style, the French Army, had been broken – as the armies of their allies of the Second and Third Coalitions against Napoleon had been broken in very comparable campaigns in 1800 and 1805. Sea-power, and air-power, enabled Britain to avoid being swept up in the general ruin and gave some hope of prolonged survival. But how could she possibly *win*? Her best chance, it was clear, lay in postponing any decisive encounter for as long as possible, while using her sea-power to build up her own strength and her air-power to erode that of the enemy. If this could be done successfully, estimated the Chiefs of Staff in the summer of 1940, the German Empire might collapse from within; the German Army, paralysed by lack of petrol and by patriot revolts in the satellite nations, might be unable to fight; and the British Army could then return to the Continent, not to force a decisive engagement with the Wehrmacht, but to receive its surrender and restore order.

This strategy of erosion and harassment was certainly in conformity with historical precedent. But in the days of Napoleon and his predecessors it had been used, either as an instrument to enforce a compromise peace, or in combination with the armies of continental allies. Now it had to be relied on to produce decisive victory on its own. The Chiefs of Staff, in the summer of 1940, professed themselves optimistic about its success. One should not judge them too harshly for this optimism: without it, they could hardly have carried on their tasks at all. At all events they reported to the Prime

Minister in May 1940 that by bombing and blockade they hoped to produce in Germany such crippling shortages of foodstuffs and oil that there would be 'widespread starvation in many of the industrial areas [of Europe] including parts of Germany, before the winter of 1940. . . . By the same date depletion of oil stocks will force Germany to weaken her military control in Europe or to immobilise her armed forces'. Under these conditions, they estimated, it would not be a difficult task to provoke occupied Europe to armed revolt by skilful subversion. By 1942, they reckoned in September 1940, conditions might be such that a British striking force 30 divisions strong would be able to establish itself on the Continent and impose its own terms.[1]

At the time, so many factors were unknown that it is not surprising that these calculations proved completely wrong. It was to be four years before strategic bombing began to produce the kind of results which its advocates had predicted. The hopes of stirring Europe to revolt rested largely on the reports of refugees, whose evidence on such questions is notoriously unreliable. In fact, outside the traditionally rebellious Balkan peninsula, subversion began to show serious results only when it became linked to the prospect of military victory for the Allies. Germany's shortage of foodstuffs and oil were real enough; but she was able to keep them from falling to the disastrous level predicted by allied intelligence, partly by seizing stocks from her defeated adversaries and partly by drawing not only on the Balkans but on Soviet Russia for supplies. There can have been few wars in which Britain's naval blockade had less hope of producing a decisive result; or in which Britain was herself more vulnerable to the counter-pressures which Germany began to exercise, through the Battle of the Atlantic, in 1941.

[1] J. R. M. Butler, *Grand Strategy* (U.K. Official History of the Second World War, Military Series, London 1957), vol. II, pp. 213–5, 343–5.

As for the resources at Britain's disposal, they were certainly considerable; but mobilizing them presented serious difficulties. So long as she 'commanded the seas', Britain could draw on the resources of her Commonwealth and Empire as well as on those of such friendly neutrals as the United States. But the maintenance of that command absorbed a high proportion of the resources which it made available. Between 1940 and 1942 the Royal Navy was, outside the Mediterranean, almost entirely a defensive force. So was the greatest part of the Army, of which nearly half had to be deployed overseas. Britain's Far Eastern possessions had to be guarded against the looming threat of Japan; and strong forces had to be retained in the Middle East, which was not only an important strategic centre for Commonwealth communications, but a source of oil even more significant for the United Kingdom than the Balkans were for Germany. The thirty divisions which the Chiefs of Staff hoped to have available to re-enter Europe in 1942 were all that could be spared for an offensive against an adversary ten times their strength and incomparably more skilful. Meanwhile, what was there available to strike at Germany, except the squadrons of Bomber Command?

But if there seemed no prospect of a successful decision against Germany herself there was a subsidiary theatre where British forces could be employed to harass the enemy and perhaps inflict serious damage. Italy's entry into the war had turned the Middle East into an active theatre of operations. As a centre of gravity for British forces it was second only to the United Kingdom itself. Egypt had been a British *place d'armes* for nearly sixty years. The establishment of British influence in the successor states to the Ottoman Empire, the development of the oil resources of Iraq and the Persian Gulf, the uneasy responsibilities of the Palestine Mandate, all had increased Britain's military involvement in the area during the years before the war. The fall of France and the belligerence of Italy eliminated the traditional rôle of the Suez Canal itself as a lifeline of the British Empire; but Egypt was still the theatre where forces could be most easily concentrated from all parts of the Commonwealth with the exception of Canada. Troops from India, Australia, New Zealand, Southern Africa and the United Kingdom could be brought into action, if not against Germany, then at least against her vulnerable ally, who could thus be turned into a liability rather than an asset to the Axis. It was an area where British and Commonwealth forces could fight on the scale to which they were accustomed, and perhaps do damage out of all proportion to their size. The defeat of Italy might influence the attitude of the French authorities in Syria, Lebanon and French North Africa. It would be taken into account in Madrid, where General Franco had it in his power to close the Mediterranean to British shipping altogether. And it would have important repercussions in the Balkan peninsula.

It was on the Balkans, indeed, that the eyes of the British authorities in Cairo had been fixed since the beginning of the war. It was only there that they could inflict direct damage on their major adversary. If Britain needed to cover the oil installations of the Persian Gulf, it was no less important for the Germans to protect those around Ploesti. On 27 May 1940, when it became clear that Allied resistance in the West had collapsed, General Wavell proposed that, since shortage of oil might be the eventual cause of Germany's defeat, the prime task of Middle Eastern Command should be to prevent Rumanian oil from reaching Germany.[1] Moreover, the Middle East itself would be threatened if a German military presence were to become established in Greece and the islands of the Aegean. In the eyes of British strategists, then as now,

[1] John Connell, *Wavell, Soldier and Scholar* (London 1965), pp. 232–3.

Greece was an essential part of the defensive complex of the Eastern Mediterranean, a Levantine rather than a Balkan state. Equally, a British presence in Greece presented no less dangerous a threat to German interests in the Balkans. In this part of the world the jugular veins of the two antagonists ran so close to one another that a struggle for mastery could hardly be avoided.

Even before Mussolini precipitated matters by his invasion of Greece in the autumn of 1940, British diplomacy had been actively seeking to build up a Balkan League of Yugoslavia, Greece and Turkey to provide a second European front. The *coup d'état* in Yugoslavia in March 1941 was a diplomatic success to which Germany felt compelled to reply by force of arms. The British attempt to counter the German invasion of Yugoslavia and Greece was a fiasco, but none of the statesmen or soldiers responsible – Mr Eden and General Sir John Dill, to whom responsibility was delegated by the War Cabinet, and General Wavell himself – doubted that the attempt had to be made. 'I am still sure,' Wavell wrote in 1950, 'that my instinct, to fight as far forward as possible in defence of the Middle East, was correct.'[1]

The hasty withdrawal of British and Commonwealth forces from Greece and Crete did not mean that the British authorities – especially those in Cairo – lost interest in the Balkan peninsula, an area so tantalizingly close and where so much damage could, with comparatively small expenditure of effort, be done. With the Yugoslav government in exile in London and the Greek in Cairo, the Foreign Office found itself deeply involved in the internal politics of those unhappy countries. In the mountains of both, resistance movements survived which needed help. Hope of winning Turkey, if not as an ally then at least as a base for operations – all the more

[1] Ibid., p. 330. For the views of Dill and Eden, see the Memoirs of Lord Avon, vol. II, *The Reckoning* (London 1965), pp. 195-8.

ter Germany invaded Russia in June 1941 – con-
scinate the Prime Minister and the Chiefs of Staff.
npts which the British had begun in 1940, to gain
reek and Yugoslav allies by diplomacy and mili-
tary assistance, were to continue almost till the end of the war.

But useful as such activities were, they could not be decisive
for the outcome of the war. Indeed in 1941 and 1942 the
British fought in the Middle East under the considerable
disadvantage that, whereas any victories they were likely to
achieve there could do only indirect damage to German
interests, an Axis victory which drove British forces from
Egypt and the Persian Gulf might make it impossible for them
to carry on the war at all – a situation which Hitler's naval
and military advisers were, happily, quite unable to make him
understand. At best, British victories in the Middle East
could only compel the diversion of German troops to the
Mediterranean – and that not in sufficient quantities to make
possible an invasion of North-West Europe. Moreover, by
the summer of 1941 it was clear that the earlier hopes built
on the probable effects of blockade and bombardment were
not likely to be fulfilled. How at this stage did the British
Chiefs of Staff, after a year of standing virtually alone against
Germany, with no expectation either of Russian or of
American armed help, think that they were going to win
the war?

In the appreciations of the Joint Planning Staff during 1941,
expectations of the economic collapse of the Third Reich
were playing a decreasingly prominent part. But hopes of its
political collapse were correspondingly growing. In the
summer of 1940 a Special Operations Executive had been
established under the control of the Minister for Economic
Warfare, Dr Hugh Dalton, who received from the Prime
Minister the laconic directive to 'set Europe ablaze'. Upon
the activities of this organization a great deal of store was

set: subversion ranked with bombing and blockade as one of the three major weapons at Britain's disposal. In March 1941 the Joint Planning Staff suggested:

We should be able overnight to produce the anarchy of Ireland in 1920 or Palestine in 1936 . . . [It would then be the rôle of British armed forces] to isolate the area from German intervention from outside, to assist the patriots in the capture of important centres and to destroy enemy formed bodies within the area. Powerful air forces will be used to interrupt the German communications and harass their troops. If we have access to the country by sea, armoured formations will be landed to strike swiftly and deep into the area. Sufficient infantry formations will be required to protect the bases and harbours on which these armoured troops depend.[1]

When they came to discuss these proposals, the Chiefs of Staff saw certain disadvantages in thus relying upon these 'secret armies' to paralyse the Wehrmacht. For one thing, to equip them on the scale that SOE considered necessary would have required a massive diversion of aircraft from the bombing offensive whose strength and achievements were already disappointing enough. For another, the effectiveness of such a rising was quite unpredictable. It could not be rehearsed, and the problems of communication and liaison would be enormous. Nevertheless the Chiefs of Staff continued to accept it as a basic principle, that the British Army should be prepared to act primarily as a detonator to this great popular upheaval. It was a central element in the strategy which they outlined to a somewhat sceptical audience when they met the US Joint Chiefs of Staff at Placentia, Newfoundland, in August 1941; and we find it again in the memorandum which Mr Churchill wrote the following December on his way to the first great Allied Conference at Washington:

[1] J. M. Gwyer and J. R. M. Butler, *Grand Strategy*, vol. III (London 1964), p. 43.

The war can only be ended through the defeat in Europe of the German Armies, or through internal convulsions in Germany produced by the unfavourable course of the war, economic privations, and the Allied bombing offensive. . . . We have therefore to prepare for the liberation of the captive countries of Western and Southern Europe by the landing at suitable points, successively or simultaneously, of British and American armies strong enough to enable the conquered populations to revolt. . . . If the incursion of the armoured formations is successful, the uprising of the local population, for whom weapons must be brought, will supply the corpus of the liberating offensive.[1]

This concept was not one of those romantic *idées fixes* which Mr Churchill's military advisers had learned to dread and which a huge amount of time and effort had to be expended to combat. It was a statement of official British strategic doctrine. But it owed little to any precedents derived from Britain's past wars. If there was a historical parallel, it was with the ideas which certain leaders of the Red Army entertained briefly in 1920-1, when they suggested that they could disregard orthodox strategic principles in an invasion of Western Europe since the appearance of Russian forces would of itself be enough to spark off the irresistible revolution of the proletariat. Like them, the British were pinning their hopes, not on a classical decisive battle, but on a mass revolt.

These hopes were not to be entirely misplaced. A popular movement of this kind did indeed liberate Yugoslavia. In North Africa, although there was little sign of 'popular revolt', the landing of Allied forces was in itself enough to swing the loyalties of the French authorities and induce them to put their resources at the invaders' disposal. The part played by the French Resistance in making possible the landings in Normandy and the rapid liberation of French territory there-

[1] Ibid., pp. 334-5.

after is seldom given enough credit by British or American military historians. But outside Yugoslavia these resistance movements never supplied 'the corpus of the liberating offensive'. British and American armies had to be landed in sufficient strength, not simply to 'enable the conquered populations to revolt', but to defeat the German forces in direct combat. The resistance movements did magnificent work, as they had in the Iberian Peninsula a century earlier, in tying down the occupying forces, cutting their communications, destroying their isolated units and harassing their retreat. But, as in the Peninsula, their activities could be effective only when they were subsidiary to those of regular troops. It was expecting too much to ask, as the British were apparently doing in 1941, for a complete reversal of rôles.

Ironically enough these ideas, revolutionary in every sense of the word, were being entertained by the Chiefs of Staff just at the moment in the history of the war when the problems which confronted them were becoming more amenable to a traditional type of solution. The Prime Minister's memorandum of December 1941 recognized that 'Hitler's failure and losses in Russia are the prime facts in the war at this time'. The Russian campaign had opened in June, six months previously, but after their lamentable showing in the Finnish operations of 1939–40 the Russian armies were not expected by many Western experts to survive the year. The initial successes of the Wehrmacht seemed to bear out the gloomiest expectations. But in November the Russians held fast before Moscow. In December they went over, successfully, to counter-attack. A new factor had appeared, of even greater significance than the entry into the war of the United States: a land army large enough to force upon the Germans a decision by battle.

This was not, however, the rôle for which the Russian Army was cast in the calculations of the British Chiefs of

Staff. The Eastern Front was not seen as a theatre where the final decision would be reached. The operations in progress there were regarded rather as a contribution to the general process of erosion and attrition to which the Third Reich was already being subjected, by air, by sea and from within. The Joint Planning Staff, preparing the British papers for the Washington Conference of December 1941, wrote:

We hope that the offensive against Germany will take the form of large-scale land operations on the Russian front, large-scale bombing operations supplemented by amphibious raids of increasing weight from the United Kingdom and a gradual tightening of the ring around Axis-controlled Europe by the occupation of strategic points in the Atlantic Islands, North and West Africa, Tripoli and Turkey. Every opportunity will be taken to try and knock out Italy as an active partner in the war. These operations will be followed in the final phase by simultaneous land operations against Germany herself, from the West by the British, from the South by the United States and from the East by the Russians.[1]

In this programme of 'tightening the ring', operations in the Mediterranean would naturally play a major part. As the conference assembled at Washington in December General Auchinleck's offensive in the Western Desert, Operation CRUSADER, was already successfully under way. This, it was hoped in London, would not only remove the threat to Egypt but eliminate Axis power from Libya, relieve the pressure on Malta, and bring a victorious army to the borders of French North Africa. Thus encouraged, the French authorities might be persuaded to open their ports to British or Anglo-American landings from the West, and with the whole southern littoral in friendly hands the Mediterranean would be open to Allied shipping.

[1] Ibid., pp. 343–4. It should be noted that at this stage the Joint Planning Staff assumed that operations through French North Africa and across the Western Mediterranean would be primarily an American responsibility.

This last advantage loomed largest in the eyes of the British Chiefs of Staff, whose resources were now overstretched by Japan's entry into the war. In addition, the blockade of Germany would be tightened; the territories, resources and manpower of the French Empire in North and West Africa would be brought into the conflict on the side of the Allies; and the vulnerable southern and south-eastern extremities of Hitler's Europe would lie open to attack by air, sea and land. General Sir Alan Brooke, the new Chief of the Imperial General Staff, summed up the position in a diary entry of 3 December 1941: 'I am positive that our policy for the conduct of the war should be to direct both military and political efforts towards the early conquest of North Africa. From there we shall be able to reopen the Mediterranean and stage offensive operations against Italy.' To which he added the later gloss: 'It was plain to me that we must clear North Africa to open the Mediterranean, and until we had done so we should never have enough shipping to stage major operations.'[1]

This strategic concept was thus not one of flexible manœuvre, or of the skilful deployment of inferior resources. Rather, it was a return to the ideas held by the British and French General Staffs at the beginning of the war: the mustering of superior resources and the isolation of the enemy, followed by a period of pressing in upon the crumbling opponent by stages not yet clearly foreseen. The most suitable historical parallel can perhaps be found, not in British military history, but in American – in the 'Anaconda' strategy adopted by Lincoln and Grant against the Confederacy in 1864, the remorseless squeezing by superior forces of an adversary cut off from outside help. Where the final break would come was not at this stage specified. The finished British memorandum which the Chiefs of Staff presented in Washington spoke

[1] Arthur Bryant, *The Turn of the Tide* (London 1957), p. 278.

only of an ultimate return to the Continent 'across the Mediterranean, from Turkey into the Balkans, or by landings in Western Europe'. It is apparent that none of the British leaders, including Churchill and Brooke, were yet prepared to recommend where and how the decision should be forced – if indeed it had to be forced at all. The prospect which they held out to their Allies was still that of the general collapse of the Third Reich under accumulated external and internal pressures. To this prospect the US Joint Chiefs of Staff raised no immediate objections. But it was not one which they were entirely happy to accept, and we must now consider wherein their hesitations lay.

# 2

## The Making of the Mediterranean Strategy, 1941-3

AT the Washington Conference the British and American Chiefs of Staff jointly agreed on a Memorandum, WW1, which defined the essential features of allied Grand Strategy.[1] Its principal points included:

(*a*) 'The realization of the victory programme of armaments, which first and foremost requires the security of the main areas of war industry.' [i.e. the United States, the United Kingdom, and Soviet Russia.]

(*b*) The maintenance of essential communications. [i.e. the defeat of the U-boats.]

(*c*) Closing and tightening the ring around Germany. [Sustaining the Russian front, arming and supporting Turkey, building up strength in the Middle East and gaining possession of the whole North African coast.]

(*d*) Wearing down and undermining German resistance by air bombardment, blockade, subversive activities and propaganda.

(*e*) The continuous development of offensive action against Germany. ['It does not seem likely that in 1942 any

[1] *Grand Strategy*, vol. III, p. 669.

large-scale land offensive against Germany will be possible. . . . In 1943 the way may be clear for a return to the Continent, across the Mediterranean, from Turkey into the Balkans, or by landings in Western Europe.']

(ƒ) 'Maintaining only such positions in the Eastern theatre as will safeguard vital interests and to deny to Japan access to raw materials vital to her continuous war effort while we are concentrating on the defeat of Germany.'

This paper followed almost word for word the draft which the British had brought with them to Washington. The Americans made only slight modifications; but they were nevertheless uneasy and during the next few months their uneasiness was to increase. The Joint Chiefs of Staff had decided as early as the previous February that, if the United States became involved in war simultaneously with Germany and with Japan, priority should be given to the defeat of Germany. With Germany beaten, the destruction of Japan would only be a matter of time; but the defeat of Japan would do nothing to enfeeble a victorious Germany. When this decision was taken, the full effect of the catastrophe at Pearl Harbor could not have been foreseen. The losses inflicted on the Pacific Fleet, the rapid seizure of the Philippines and the establishment of a ring of island bases protecting the new Great East Asia Co-Prosperity Sphere made the defeat of Japan a far more complicated and expensive business than had ever been conceived; while the humiliations inflicted on American arms created strong public pressure to avenge them as rapidly as possible. Understanding between the US Army and the US Navy authorities was something less than perfect, and the Navy was both by tradition and by necessity predominantly concerned with the Pacific Ocean, where it had such heavy tasks and crushing responsibilities. When it came to the allocation of resources between the Pacific and the

European theatres, therefore, the Joint Chiefs of Staff found it very difficult indeed to maintain in its pristine purity the doctrine of 'Germany First'.

Under these circumstances it is not surprising that the United States Army Planning Staff considered British strategic plans for the defeat of Germany to be leisurely and indecisive. They were particularly unsympathetic to the view which the Chiefs of Staff put forward at Placentia, that the war could be won without the German armies being met and defeated in the field. On this the US Joint Board had commented curtly, 'It should be recognized as an almost invariable rule that wars cannot finally be won without the use of land armies'. As a result of this belief, the US Army set on foot, even before the United States entered the war, a programme of expansion designed to increase its strength from 40 underequipped to 200 divisions.[1] Further, its Operations and Plans Staff had worked out where these forces could best be brought to bear, and identified the plains of North-West Europe as the main theatre 'where we must come to grips with the enemy ground forces'. All other theatres, not only in the Far East but in Europe as well, were downgraded as 'subsidiary'.[2] The United States Army still held to the clear and simple principles which had guided European strategists before 1914: mobilize the greatest possible resources, concentrate them as quickly as possible at the decisive point, and there engage in battle to settle the matter.

But like European strategists before them, they found that this was easier said than done. Once war began China, Australasia, the Central Pacific, the Western Hemisphere itself, the Atlantic, the Mediterranean, the Middle East, the

---

[1] Ibid., p. 143, quoting M. S. Watson, *Chief of Staff: Pre-War Plans and Preparations*, pp. 238, 343-5, 358.

[2] Maurice Matloff and Edwin Snell, *Strategic Planning for Coalition Warfare 1941-42* (Washington 1953), p. 101.

Soviet Union and the United Kingdom were all clamouring for the resources which the American cornucopia was only just beginning to produce. Within a month of the Washington Conference, on 22 January 1942, we find General Dwight D. Eisenhower, Chief of the US Army Operations and Planning Staff, writing:

We've got to go to Europe and fight – and we've got to quit wasting resources all over the world – and still worse – wasting time. If we're to keep Russia in, save the Middle East, India and Burma, we've got to begin slugging with air at West Europe; to be followed by a land attack as soon as possible.[1]

American and British military authorities, in fact, approached the problem of devising a strategy for the defeat of Germany from different ends. The British began with mobilization and deployment of forces, assuming that circumstances would determine where the decisive engagement would occur – if indeed any such clear 'decision', easily identifiable in time and space, proved necessary at all. Their philosophy was Napoleonic: '*on s'engage et puis on voit.*' The Americans, on the other hand, started by deciding where the decisive engagement should occur, worked back from there to their plans for deployment, and from there to mobilization of resources. Only if they knew what kind of war they were going to fight, they argued with some reason, could they decide what kind of weapons to procure and what kind of forces to raise. It was this difference in approach, and not any conflict between 'manœuvre' and 'mass', that underlay most of the subsequent disputes between the Allies over strategic planning. In the view of the British, American eyes were so firmly fixed on the ultimate objective that they overlooked most of the problems of actually getting there – the basic but

[1] Ibid., p. 156.

unprecedented logistical difficulties of landing and deploying large forces on an enemy-held land mass. They also considered that the Americans underestimated the necessity, which they themselves had learned the hard way in Norway, Belgium and Greece, of engaging the Wehrmacht only in the most favourable circumstances possible; in particular with an overwhelming local superiority of force and with command of the air. In return, the Americans considered the British strategy to be indecisive and peripheral, haunted by memories of the slaughters in the First World War, and of early defeats in the Second. They doubted whether Britain's military leaders, even Churchill himself, staunch as they were in defence, were prepared to make the sacrifices necessary for a victorious attack; and as the war went on their doubts did not decrease.

Neither criticism was entirely unfounded. The original American proposals for the invasion of North-West Europe displayed a certain naïveté. General Marshall was later to confess that before the war he had never heard of any landing craft except a rubber boat. His military education, he told Marshal Voroshilov at Teheran, 'had been based on roads, rivers and railroads . . . during the last two years he had been acquiring an education based on oceans and he had to learn all over again.'[1] As for the British, they did not conceal their reluctance to repeat the experiences of Passchendaele and the Somme. Their army did not have the size, and perhaps did not have the *morale*, to stand heavy casualties. Trained in small-scale operations, it had difficulty in adjusting itself to the necessity for large-scale land war, and attaining the requisite standard of expertise. Once engaged in action the caution of commanders laudably determined not to repeat the butcheries of 1914-18, its lavish use of artillery to avoid

[1] Robert S. Sherwood, *The White House Papers of Harry Hopkins* (London 1948), vol. II, p. 778.

casualties and the reluctance of its infantry to engage in close combat were commented on by ally and enemy alike.[1]

There was a further reason why the Americans hesitated to accept British plans. The US Army Planning Staff drew a sharp distinction between the United Kingdom itself, which they were prepared to defend, and 'British interests' – particularly British Imperial interests – which they were not. As early as the autumn of 1940 they had feared that 'as the danger to the British Isles becomes less acute, to support Great Britain might well amount to supporting, at first indirectly and then directly, British positions throughout the world – in short to acquiesce in British grand strategy'.[2] They observed that 'British deployments and operations apparently were undertaken primarily with a view to maintaining the integrity of the British Empire'.[3] They did not want to become drawn into protecting British possessions and interests, either in the Far East or in the Middle East, and operations which derived their rationale from Britain's position in the latter theatre awoke their immediate suspicions. Operations in the Mediterranean and the Balkans were thus peculiarly suspect to them. The arguments which the British advanced at Washington in favour of landings in French North Africa were denounced by one senior US Army Planner as 'persuasive rather than rational', and were generally believed in the War Department to be 'motivated more largely by political than by sound strategic purposes'.[4] There was a very strong fear in influential American quarters that American soldiers were being cozened into picking British political chestnuts out of the fire. Nowhere is this more frankly expressed than in the account which General

[1] For a German report bearing on this question, see Marshal of the R.A.F. Lord Tedder, *With Prejudice* (London 1966), pp. 570–1.

[2] Matloff and Snell, op. cit., p. 21.

[3] Ibid., p. 243.

[4] Ibid., pp. 104–5.

Albert C. Wedemeyer, then a senior officer on General Marshall's Operations and Planning Staff, gives in his memoirs of the staff conferences in London in April 1942:

The British were masters in negotiations – particularly were they adept in the use of phrases or words which were capable of more than one interpretation. Here was the setting, with all the trappings of a classical Machiavellian scene. I am not suggesting that the will to deceive was a personal characteristic of any of the participants. But when matters of state were involved, our British opposite numbers had elastic scruples. To skirt the facts for King and Country was justified in the consciences of these British gentlemen. . . . What I witnessed was the British power of finesse in its finest hour, a power that had been developed over centuries of successful international intrigue, cajolery and tacit compulsions. . . . It is true, I thought, that the sun never sets on the British Empire. But neither does the dove of peace. Moreover, the wings of justice had constantly been clipped as British influence and possessions were increased all over the world.[1]

General Wedemeyer's views should not, perhaps, be regarded as entirely typical; but the fact that they could be entertained at all by an officer of his seniority and influence does something to explain why United States planners were not always prepared to accept British proposals at their face value. The cordial relations established between many influential individuals on both sides of the Atlantic on which historians of both countries have dwelt with such justifiable satisfaction – pre-eminently the friendship between General Marshall and the British military representative on the Combined Chiefs of Staff, Field Marshal Sir John Dill – could not entirely eliminate the stubborn suspicions which lingered in military circles in Washington, that the Americans were somehow being made tools by their sophisticated and politically skilful allies.

[1] Albert C. Wedemeyer, *Wedemeyer Reports!* (New York 1958), pp. 105–6.

[25]

The American military authorities thus accepted the British proposals, and set their hands to WW1, with a number of unspoken reservations. The proposals were all right so far as they went, but they went neither far nor fast enough. As General Eisenhower pointed out, a very much firmer directive, laying down more precise priorities, was needed if resources were not to be dissipated as fast as they were produced. On 25 March 1942 he drafted such a directive himself. It decreed an immediate concentration of effort on North-West Europe, and was approved by General Marshall and President Roosevelt the same day. Two days later Eisenhower laid before General Marshall a specific plan to implement this directive. The United States was to begin forthwith to concentrate in the United Kingdom a force which, together, with those provided by the British and their other Allies would by the spring of 1943 total 48 divisions and 5,800 aircraft – Operation BOLERO. Operations to obtain command of the air over North-West Europe were also to be set on foot, as was an active policy of amphibious raids on enemy-held coasts; all leading up to an invasion a year later, in April 1943 (Operation ROUNDUP). Simultaneously a smaller operation should be prepared, for the invasion of the Continent in such force as could be made available in the summer of 1942, if German collapse made it possible or Russian collapse made it necessary (Operation SLEDGEHAMMER). American planners recognized that, since they would be able to provide for this latter operation at most only 4 divisions and 700 aircraft, responsibility for its execution would have to lie predominantly with the British.

To these plans both General Marshall and President Roosevelt gave their immediate consent. Rather than route it through the cumbrous apparatus of the Combined Chiefs of Staff, Marshall decided to present it to the British Chiefs of Staff in person, and on 8 April he flew to London to do so. By

14 April, after the discussions which made so disagreeable an impression on General Wedemeyer, the American proposal, justly described by Mr Churchill as 'momentous', had been approved, not only by the British Chiefs of Staff, but by the Defence Committee of the Cabinet. Between the initial conception of the plan and its final and formal acceptance, barely three weeks had passed.

For the British did finally and formally accept the proposal, and there is no evidence even of private doubts or *arrières pensées* on the part of the Chiefs of Staff. The only reservation they made was that sufficient forces must be kept to guard the Middle East and the Indian Ocean; the latter at the time being directly menaced by the irruption of a Japanese naval force into the Bay of Bengal. 'We whole-heartedly agree with your conception of concentration against the main enemy and we cordially accept your plan with [this] one broad qualification',[1] Mr Churchill cabled to the President. The Chiefs of Staff made clear their reservations about the possibility of mounting Operation SLEDGEHAMMER in 1942; but General Brooke noted in his diary: 'We accepted their proposals for offensive action in Europe in 1942 perhaps, and in 1943 for certain.'[2]

It may seem curious that the British should have accepted General Marshall's plan so promptly, and without subjecting it to thorough examination by their planning staffs. The US Army official history itself points out that 'only the most hurried and superficial investigation of the complex logistic problems involved had been made before the London conference, and the conference contributed very little to an understanding of them or to agreement about them. Everything remained to be done.'[3] It may have been the difference

---

[1] Winston S. Churchill, *The Second World War*, vol. IV (London 1951), p. 286.

[2] Arthur Bryant, *The Turn of the Tide*, p. 355.

[3] Matloff and Snell, op. cit., p. 191.

between this ready endorsement and the subsequent delays that led General Wedemeyer to write of these April meetings as bitterly as he did. But the American proposals did not conflict with the British plans as outlined in WWI. These had not only visualized a return to the Continent in 1943, but had indicated Western Europe as one of the areas where this might take place. Operations in the Mediterranean were still considered by the Chiefs of Staff in terms of clearing the North African coast and releasing shipping – 'tightening the ring'. Besides, the British Joint Planning Staff had themselves been considering, very seriously indeed, the idea of a cross-Channel operation in 1942. In March they had informed the Chiefs of Staff that:

Our greatest contribution to a German defeat would be the creation of a major diversion in the West designed to upset German plans and divert German forces from the East. Lack of shipping precludes the strategy of such a diversion anywhere except across the Channel.[1]

and on 6 April the Chiefs of Staff cabled to the Joint Staff Mission in Washington:

We consider that the importance of helping Russia in 1942 is so great that the consideration of an offensive in 1943 should not prevent us from doing anything we can, however small, this summer.[2]

General Marshall's proposal thus came as no surprise to the British. In the terrible three months that had followed Japan's entry into the war, with the Far East collapsing, the Indian Ocean threatened and U-boat operations in the Atlantic growing ever more intensive, the British Chiefs of Staff had had little chance to think about the eventual form of the offensive; but the American plan did not conflict in any

[1] *Grand Strategy*, vol. III, p. 567.
[2] Ibid., p. 573.

essentials with such ideas as they had entertained. There would certainly have been little inclination on their part to rebuff, by an untimely examination of minutiae, so emphatic a reassertion of the principle of 'Europe First', at a moment when the Americans were under strong pressure to abandon it; but the evidence suggests that both Mr Churchill and his Chiefs of Staff were, in April 1942, entirely sincere in their acceptance of the BOLERO–ROUND-UP plan as expounded by General Marshall, and were determined to put it into effect. There was certainly not, at that time, any alternative and conflicting 'Mediterranean strategy'.

Throughout the spring of 1942 the British and the Americans were thus in complete agreement about their Grand Strategy. General Eisenhower himself was put in command of the United States forces which almost immediately began to cross the Atlantic to the United Kingdom. Careful studies were conducted in London as to the practicability of Operation SLEDGEHAMMER; but about ROUND-UP no doubts were expressed at all. When General Brooke visited Washington with the Prime Minister in June, he explicitly agreed with his American colleagues that no operation should be undertaken in 1942 which should prejudice the chances of ROUND-UP in 1943. A landing in French North Africa was in fact singled out as being such a rival operation. Rather than that, the Combined Chiefs of Staff agreed on 21 June, they would recommend attacks against Brest, against the Channel Islands, or even against Norway. 'In our view,' they agreed, 'each would be accompanied by certain hazards that would be justified only by reasons that were compelling in nature. Any of these plans, however, would be preferable to undertaking GYMNAST [landings in French North Africa], especially from the standpoint of dispersing base organisation, lines of sea communication, and air strength.'[1] General Brooke indeed,

[1] Ibid., p. 626. Matloff and Snell, op. cit., p. 239.

in his diary entry for 20 June, went so far as to bracket a North African operation with one in North Norway as being 'not possible'.[1]

Meanwhile, the British staff officers studying Operation SLEDGEHAMMER had come to the decision that that was not possible either. No operation, they considered, could be launched, with the forces available in the summer of 1942, that stood any chance of establishing a beach-head which could not be rapidly eliminated by the German forces already stationed in North-West Europe. This unwelcome news was personally reported to the President by Vice-Admiral Lord Louis Mountbatten, the Chief of Combined Operations. General Eisenhower was most unwilling to accept it; but his unwillingness, as he later admitted, derived not from any disagreement of substance, but from his sharing with his colleagues 'a lively suspicion that the British contemplated the agreed-on cross-Channel concept with distaste'. Subsequent developments, he confessed, convinced him 'that those who held the SLEDGEHAMMER operation to be unwise at the moment were correct in their evaluation of the problem';[2] a judgement from which few, after the Dieppe raid in August 1942, would be likely to dissent. Since this operation would have to be carried out mainly with British forces, the British veto was absolute.

But President Roosevelt was equally determined that an operation of some kind must be launched by American forces in the European theatre in 1942. He had given M. Molotov an unwisely specific assurance that a Second Front in Europe would be opened in 1942; and during the last week in June the Germans had opened their summer offensive, with a success almost as spectacular as that which their armies had enjoyed the previous year. Something apparently had

[1] Arthur Bryant, *The Turn of the Tide*, p. 403.
[2] Dwight D. Eisenhower, *Crusade in Europe* (London 1948), p. 79.

to be done to avert a total Russian collapse. But something had to be done also to get the American public emotionally involved in the European theatre for which so many of them had scant sympathy at a time when their attention was naturally focused on the Pacific. 'U.S. ground forces', the President therefore ordered, 'must be put into position to fight German ground forces somewhere in 1942.'[1]

This was the context in which Mr Churchill again brought forward the proposal for Allied landings in French North Africa. The idea had, as we have seen, been considered at the Washington Conference the previous December but had been allowed to lapse. Shortage of shipping, combined with the rebuff to the Eighth Army in the Western Desert, had made it clearly impracticable. But the President had remained favourably inclined to the proposal, and the reports which he was getting from the US consular authorities in Algeria indicated that the French authorities themselves might be induced to welcome it, or be rapidly replaced from within if they did not. Mr Churchill's own advocacy of the operation, and of its subsequent exploitation, has appeared to some historians to derive from an obsession with indirect strategy in general and the Mediterranean in particular; an obsession perhaps originating with the failure of the Dardanelles expedition, with which his name was so closely associated, during the First World War. Such a hypothesis can be neither proved nor disproved; but it seems an unnecessarily complicated and far-fetched explanation for the revival of a project which fitted quite naturally into the pattern of 'closing the ring' agreed by the Combined Chiefs of Staff six months before. It may be suggested that even if Mr Churchill had had no hand whatever in the Dardanelles expedition he would have revived the idea of Operation GYMNAST, and that if he had not done so

[1] Sherwood, *The White House Papers of Harry Hopkins*, vol. II, p. 607.

someone else would. Given that a major operation had to be launched in the European Theatre in 1942, no other could be suggested – or rather, no other *was* suggested – which offered the slightest hope of success.

The American Joint Chiefs of Staff continued to resist the proposal, and it took a direct order from the President to make them accept it. For they realized, as did the British Chiefs of Staff, that in order to mount the operation on the necessary scale, it would be necessary to divert resources from Operation BOLERO to such an extent that ROUND-UP would not be possible at all in 1943. This was something which it took Mr Churchill many months to understand. 'It should not be admitted', he directed, 'that GYMNAST, though it impinges temporarily upon BOLERO, is at the expense of ROUND-UP.'[1] The Americans were under no such illusions. General Eisenhower, seeing all his plans collapse, feared that the decision to launch Operation TORCH (as it was now renamed) might mark 'the blackest day in history'.[2] General Marshall more soberly considered it 'a momentous change in Grand Strategy'.[3] The immediate impulse of his staff, to abandon the 'Europe First' concept altogether, was sharply suppressed by the President; but the decisive change had nevertheless been made. For the US Army, as we have seen, concentration on Europe had meant concentration on the North Atlantic theatre. The Mediterranean for them was as subsidiary as the Pacific. Once that ruling principle, established by Eisenhower in March, had been abandoned, the 'dissipation' of resources which he so much dreaded could not be checked. For the rest of the year resources flowed as fast to the Pacific – where the struggle for the Solomon Islands had begun in August – as they did to

[1] *Grand Strategy*, vol. III, p. 638.
[2] Harry S. Butcher, *My Three Years with Eisenhower* (London 1946), p. 29.
[3] Matloff and Snell, op. cit., p. 294.

the Mediterranean, while those to the United Kingdom died to a trickle.

General Marshall spelled out the full implications of this change in a document of 24 July to which the British Chiefs of Staff, perhaps anxious to avoid further controversy, also set their hand. 'A commitment to GYMNAST,' this stated, 'implies the definite acceptance of a defensive, encircling line of action for the Continental European Theatre, except as to air and blockade operations against Germany.'[1] This was not closing the ring as the British saw it – a preliminary step to the garrotting of the Third Reich. It was cordoning off Germany in exactly the same way as the British intended Japan to be cordoned off; by the establishment of a defensive perimeter to prevent the adversary from doing further harm while more decisive operations were carried out elsewhere. This concept was reflected in American strategy for the conquest of North Africa, which contemplated primarily a landing on the Atlantic coast and the gradual establishment of Allied influence throughout Morocco and Algeria. The British desire for landings as far east as possible, to gain rapid control of the vital Tunisian straits, was regarded with little sympathy in Washington, and only the personal intervention of Mr Churchill with President Roosevelt brought the Americans to agree to landings even as far east as Algiers. There were other reasons for American hesitations – shortage of shipping, mistrust of Spanish intentions, and reluctance to commit their unblooded troops to too ferocious an initiation; but it was natural enough that they should be unwilling to run too many risks in establishing 'a defensive encircling line'.

For the British, however, the opening of operations in the Western Mediterranean was no more a 'defensive' movement than is that of a hangman slipping a noose over the head of a

[1] *Grand Strategy*, vol. III, p. 635.

condemned man. The ring was to be closed, and then tightened. One can, however, trace a divergence of view between Mr Churchill and his Chiefs of Staff over the significance of operations in the Mediterranean and what was to happen once the North African coast was cleared. Mr Churchill himself did see future operations in terms of the 'flexible manœuvres' which he read, perhaps a little too readily, into the history of Britain's previous wars. To Stalin he justified the concentration in the Mediterranean by the unfortunate analogy of an attack on the 'soft underbelly' of a crocodile: a concept which, however justifiable it may have been as an expedient for mollifying his suspicious ally, had played no part whatever in the decision to launch Operation TORCH. To his Chiefs of Staff shortly afterwards he held out a yet more glittering prospect.

If . . . we move northward into Europe, a new situation must be surveyed. The flank attack may become the main attack, and the main attack a holding operation in the early stages. Our second front will, in fact, comprise both the Atlantic and Mediterranean coasts of Europe, and we can push either right-handed, left-handed, or both-handed as our resources and circumstances permit.[1]

This last sentence was to prove a remarkably far-sighted summary of what was actually to occur and shows Churchill's opportunistic strategic thinking at its best. But even at its best, this thinking underrated the logistical difficulties of mounting any attacks on Europe, whether from south, west or north; and these were the problems which inescapably dominated the thinking of the Chiefs of Staff and their planners. Throughout the autumn of 1942 they were working out a strategy for the defeat of Germany which could develop out of the landings in North Africa: a strategy sufficiently

[1] Ibid., pp. 637–8.

attractive to persuade the Americans to abandon their concept of a 'defensive encircling line' and return to the agreed programme of WWI. Their plans were agreed only after acrimonious inter-Service disputes and often in face of strong resistance from the Prime Minister himself;[1] but agreed they were, and at the Casablanca Conference in January 1943 the US Joint Chiefs of Staff were persuaded to accept them. 'The Mediterranean Strategy' was in gestation between September and December 1942; at Casablanca it was born and legitimized.

This strategy was one not of manoeuvre, but of attrition. The Combined Chiefs of Staff agreed that the Mediterranean should be fully opened in order to release shipping resources, and to provide bases from which Allied bombers could attack new areas of the German-controlled economy. They agreed that operations should be continued to distract German strength from the Russian front, to wear down the German war machine in general, and in particular to force the collapse of Italy. They agreed on the invasion of Sicily as the measure most likely to fulfil all these objectives; but beyond that no plans were made. At this stage both General Brooke and the Joint Planning Staff were very reluctant indeed to get drawn into a land campaign in Italy itself. It was assumed, with good reason, that once the Mediterranean had been opened and Sicily taken – and perhaps Sardinia and Corsica as well – the weight of Allied sea and air power would be enough in themselves to force an Italian collapse. This would compel the Germans to take over not only the Italian mainland but also the extensive Italian commitments in the Balkan peninsula and the Aegean. The whole Mediterranean would be turned

---

[1] A full account of these disputes will be found in the author's forthcoming volume in the U.K. Official History of the Second World War, *Grand Strategy*, vol. IV, which also documents the statements and quotations contained in the next few pages.

into 'a heavy liability' for Germany, who would be compelled to divert forces both from the Eastern front and from North-West Europe. Thus immediate help would be given to the Russians, and the way would be paved for cross-Channel operation in 1944. The object agreed at Casablanca was that of 'defeating Germany in 1943 with the maximum forces that can be brought to bear upon her by the United Nations'. The hope was still there of forcing a general collapse by overall attrition; failing that, a decisive attack would be launched in 1944.

Three aspects of this 'Mediterranean strategy' must be stressed. First, it was largely opportunistic. Substantial British and American forces had been directed to French North Africa for reasons as much political as military. President Roosevelt was determined, for domestic purposes, to commit substantial forces to the European Theatre in 1942. An equally substantial British force was available in the Middle East. There was neither the time nor the shipping available to transfer these troops to Europe to launch a cross-Channel operation in 1943; so unless they were to remain idle for a year while the Russians continued to fight single-handed, some employment had to be found for them in the Mediterranean Theatre. Secondly, the Combined Chiefs did not see the Mediterranean as a 'soft underbelly' through which Europe could be invaded, but as an area where the Germans could be brought to battle: not under particularly favourable circumstances, perhaps, but a great deal more favourable than the beaches of North-West Europe. And thirdly there was as yet no question whatever of 'forestalling' the Russians, or conducting a strategy based on political foresight. The attention of all, soldiers and statesmen alike, was riveted on helping the Russians and winning the war; and there was, in 1943, no other theatre where this could be done.

Three months after the Casablanca Conference, in May

1943, the Combined Chiefs met again in Washington for their third conference – TRIDENT. As the British delegation crossed the Atlantic in the *Queen Mary*, reports were coming in of the final operations as General Alexander's forces liquidated the last Axis resistance in North Africa. The Mediterranean was open, and Italy was known to be on the verge of collapse. In the exhilaration of victory the British were now prepared to put forward ambitious plans for exploiting success. Their caution about becoming involved in land operations in Italy was apparently forgotten. The proposals which the Joint Planning Staff now presented were for the immediate and whole-hearted exploitation of General Alexander's spectacular success. The invasion of Sicily, they recommended, should be followed at once by landings in Calabria. From there the Allies should exploit eastward into the Balkans; but if meanwhile there was a total collapse of Italian resistance, Italy should be occupied as far north as Rome, a bridgehead should be established on the Dalmatian coast, the Dodecanese should be seized and Turkey pressed yet more strongly to enter the war. The Germans would be compelled to divert forces, either to the Balkan peninsula or to Italy, and since they were not thought to have the strength effectively to protect both they were likely to abandon the latter. The final conclusion of the Joint Planners was that the Mediterranean offered opportunities for action in the coming autumn and winter which might be decisive, and at the very least would do far more to prepare the way for a successful cross-Channel operation in 1944 than could be achieved by attempting to transfer back to the UK any of the forces in the Mediterranean theatre.

These proposals were accepted by the British Chiefs of Staff, who urged them on their American allies. But throughout the summer of 1943 this natural desire to exploit success had to contend with a renewed determination on the part of

General Marshall to reassert the primacy of Operation ROUND-UP – or that reduced version of it which was all that would now be possible after so many forces had been siphoned off to the Mediterranean and the Pacific. The Joint Chiefs of Staff were brought to acquiesce in further operations in the Mediterranean largely by the repeated assurance of General Brooke that only thus could the conditions be created for a successful invasion of North-West Europe. The theatre was to be regarded as subsidiary, and ancillary to what was now meaningfully re-christened Operation OVERLORD. The Americans insisted further that firm agreement over the date of that Operation must now be reached – 1 May 1944 – and that forces must be irrevocably set aside for it; including seven divisions withdrawn from the Mediterranean theatre. Without such guarantees being given, General Marshall feared a continued sapping of Allied forces without any decisive result.

With the principle clearly established at the TRIDENT Conference, that Mediterranean operations were subsidiary to OVERLORD, the precise direction that they should take became a matter of secondary importance. It was agreed simply that General Eisenhower should 'mount such operations in exploitation of HUSKY [the invasion of Sicily] as are best calculated to eliminate Italy from the war and to contain the maximum number of German forces'. The British proposals were neither endorsed nor rejected. In General Eisenhower's own headquarters they were keenly debated. If the strategic function of the Allied forces in the Mediterranean was to hold the Germans down and distract them from the Eastern and Western fronts, it was arguable that this could be done quite as effectively by seizing Corsica and Sardinia, thus threatening the Axis defences throughout the Western Mediterranean, as it could by getting involved in a land campaign on the Italian mainland in the unfavourable circumstances against which the British planners had themselves warned only a few months ago.

By now, however, few British voices were raised against the invasion of Italy, and most were thundering insistently for it. The Joint Planning Staff saw it as the best way to exploit the resistance in the Balkans, reports of which were increasing as Italy's hold on the area slackened after her African defeats. The Royal Air Force coveted the bases on the Italian mainland from which they could reach Central and South-Eastern Europe. The Chiefs of Staff pointed out to Washington a week before the invasion that the advantages of occupying as much as possible of southern Italy, even if they had to fight hard for it, would far outweigh any accruing from the capture of Sardinia, since they would be containing far greater German forces on the mainland than in Sardinia; which should be the primary consideration in determining what operation to undertake.

As for Mr Churchill himself, and perhaps for the commanders of the victorious British armies in Africa, the impulse to carry the battle into Italy was emotional as well as strategic. The Prime Minister confessed quite frankly that 'he passionately wanted to see Italy out of the war and Rome in our possession'. 'Compelling or inducing Italy to quit the war is the only objective in the Mediterranean worthy of the famous campaign already begun and adequate to the Allied forces available and already in the Mediterranean basin,' he wrote on 31 May.[1] 'For this purpose the taking of Sicily is an indispensable preliminary and the invasion of the mainland of Italy and the capture of Rome are the evident steps.' If the Germans reacted strongly, so much the better: 'we shall certainly have achieved part of our task in drawing . . . forces off our Russian allies.' As soon as the Washington Conference was over he flew to Algiers to urge these arguments on

[1] Churchill, *The Second World War*, vol. IV, p. 735.

[39]

General Eisenhower. To his confidant General Smuts he wrote, on 15 July, still more frankly: 'I will in no circumstances allow the powerful British and British-controlled armies in the Mediterranean to stand idle. . . . I shall go to all lengths to procure the agreement of our Allies. If not, we have ample forces to act by ourselves.' The prestige of British arms, it appears, demanded that the triumphal progress of the Eighth Army must continue, unchecked by the cold calculations of planners in Washington.

It is not surprising that such an attitude did not impress General Marshall, who accompanied the Prime Minister to Algiers. But there were stronger arguments than this for launching the Italian campaign, as we have seen above, and they found support among the American as well as the British members of General Eisenhower's staff. The outcome of the discussion at Algiers was that General Eisenhower set up two planning groups, to prepare simultaneously for the two alternative possibilities: an attack on Sardinia, and a landing in Southern Italy. The curious situation obtained, therefore, that when the Allied armies landed in Sicily on 10 July, nobody had yet decided where they were to go next.

# 3

## The Invasion of Southern Europe, 1943-4

THE Allied invasion of Sicily came as the *coup de grâce* to an Italy whose armies had been defeated and in large part captured; whose overseas Empire had been lost; whose cities and communications were being hammered from the air; and whose population was unanimous in longing for the end of the war. Only in a very few cases did the Italian forces in Sicily attempt serious resistance. Throughout the Balkan peninsula and the Aegean Islands Italian garrisons signalled to partisans their desire to surrender. The senior officers of the Army, under the leadership of General Ambrosio, the Chief of the General Staff, presented to Mussolini a virtual ultimatum demanding the opening of peace negotiations, and on 17 July the Duce travelled north to meet Hitler at Feltre and make Italy's parlous position perfectly clear. Hitler refused to listen; and since it was now evident that Mussolini would not take Italy out of the war on his own account, his subordinates resolved to do so themselves. The Army leaders joined forces with the conspirators around the royal court whose plans and resolution had been growing firmer throughout the summer, and on 24 July Mussolini was overthrown. Three weeks later General Castellano flew to Lisbon to open formal negotiations with the Allies on behalf of the new régime.

None of this surprised the German High Command, which had been quietly making plans to deal with this contingency for some two months past. Four days after Mussolini's fall, on 28 July, these were given final shape as Operation AXIS, the execution of which was entrusted to General Rommel. Throughout August German divisions seeped over the frontier into Northern Italy. By 9 September, when the Italian government announced its surrender and the Allied Fifth Army landed in the Bay of Salerno, their number had risen to fourteen, drawn in equal part from the Eastern Front and from North-West Europe. By the end of October they totalled twenty-five; more than enough to pacify the country and compel the Allies to fight hard for every yard of their advance on Rome.

But it was not Italy that caused Hitler most concern. 'If the worst comes to the worst,' he had told his advisers on 14 May, 'the Italian peninsula can be sealed off somehow. It is of decisive importance for us to hold the Balkans: oil, copper, bauxite, chrome, above all security, so that there is not a complete smash there if things get worse in Italy.'[1] The expectation of the British Joint Planning Staff, that Germany would not have sufficient forces to occupy both Italy and the Balkan peninsula, proved false. By the end of 1943, in addition to the twenty-five German divisions in Italy, there was the equivalent of a further twenty in Yugoslavia, Greece and the islands of the Aegean.[2] But these detachments had been made only on Hitler's insistence, against the strong advice of his military staff. General Jodl, at his wit's end to find men to meet increasing pressure at every point in Germany's defences, had urged a shortening of the line in the Mediterranean. He recommended that the Italian peninsula should be abandoned south of the easily defensible mountain line between Pisa and Rimini, and in Greece and the Aegean nothing should be

[1] Führer Naval Conferences, 14 May 1943.
[2] *Kriegstagebuch der Oberkommando der Wehrmacht*, ed. Helmuth Greiner and Percy Schramm (Frankfurt A.M. 1963), vol. III, p. 1562.

held south of a line running east and west through Salonika. The Germans would thus be defending, in the Balkan peninsula, the line which the Central Powers had held very successfully during the First World War. Even if the British did make a lodgement in Thrace there was no reason to expect it to be any more of a threat to the German position than the Anglo-French position at Salonika had been twenty-five years before.

Hitler's reluctance to listen to these proposals was strengthened by the views of General Kesselring, who commanded German forces in Sicily and South Italy. A withdrawal to the Apennines, Kesselring pointed out, would not only uncover the Balkans to an Allied thrust across the Adriatic; it would make available for the Allied Combined Bomber Offensive the complex of airfields in south-east Italy around Foggia, whose value to the Allies he as an airman understood very well. Italy should therefore be defended as far forward as possible – a view shared by Admiral Dönitz, to whose advice on questions of Grand Strategy Hitler was paying increasing attention. Hitler delayed a final decision on the matter. Until the Allied landings at Salerno actually occurred, all German plans were made on the assumption that German troops would be withdrawn to the north as quickly as possible – if only because their communications, if they remained in the south, would be at the mercy of their equivocal allies. It was only in the last two weeks of September that Hitler made up his mind to fight south of Rome. The complete success of Operation AXIS, the collapse of all Italian resistance to their former ally, the ponderous slowness of the Allied advance on Naples, all this made a campaign in South Italy appear feasible. At the same time Hitler ordered that there should be no withdrawal in the Aegean. At whatever cost in men, the islands were to be held, and those lost in the Dodecanese to British *coups de main* had to be recaptured. The familiar note sounded by the Führer, directing that not a yard of ory was to be yielded, and was received by OKW with their usual exasperated acquiescence. 'Hitler's Mediterranean strategy,' General Warlimont was to write after the war, 'threw a far greater strain upon the German war potential than the military situation justified.'[1] By his decision to commit the maximum available resources to the defence of the Mediterranean, Hitler thus played into the Allied hands.

Meanwhile the uncertainties of the Allied High Command as to the future course of their own operations had been resolved by the complete and immediate collapse of the Italian forces in Sicily. The decisive voice was now to be that of General Marshall. Marshall had never been hostile to an Italian campaign as such. He had only a very natural reluctance to become involved in any further open-ended commitments which might prejudice the prospects of OVERLORD. Now the disintegration of Italian military resistance, and the rumours of Italian political collapse removed his doubts, and he found himself apparently in whole-hearted agreement with Mr Churchill. On 13 July the Prime Minister addressed to the Chiefs of Staff a note couched in a stimulating mixture of metaphors.

Why should we crawl up the leg like a harvest bug from the ankle upwards? Let us rather strike at the knee. . . . Tell the Planners to throw their hat over the fence; they need not be afraid there will not be plenty of dead weight to clog it.

On 16 July General Marshall brought forward a similar proposal to the Combined Chiefs of Staff: General Eisenhower should be urged to mount an amphibious operation to capture Naples, and then to press on as fast as possible to Rome. The Combined Chiefs of Staff endorsed this recom-

[1] Walter Warlimont, *Inside Hitler's Headquarters* (London 1964), p. 387.

mendation, and General Eisenhower was directed to begin planning for Operation AVALANCHE immediately.

But agreement over the operation itself concealed deep underlying differences over its purpose. For General Marshall Operation AVALANCHE was the most effective way of using the limited forces allocated to General Eisenhower to fulfil the objectives laid down at the Casablanca and the Washington Conferences: to knock Italy out of the war and turn the Mediterranean into a heavy liability for the Germans. For Mr Churchill, however, it was the opening up of splendid new opportunities which might even take precedence over OVERLORD. On 19 July he told the Chiefs of Staff Committee:

I have no doubt myself that the right strategy for 1944 is maximum post-HUSKY, certainly to the Po, with option to attack westward in the South of France or north-eastward towards Vienna, and meanwhile to procure the expulsion of the enemy from the Balkans and Greece. I do not believe that 27 Anglo-American divisions are sufficient for OVERLORD in view of the extraordinary fighting efficiency of the German Army and the much larger forces they could so readily bring to bear against our troops even if the landings were successfully accomplished.[1]

It seemed to at least one well-placed American observer at this time that there was a general weakening in the British determination to carry out OVERLORD. Mr Henry L. Stimson, Secretary for the Army, was visiting London and on returning to Washington he reported his impressions frankly to the President:

We cannot now rationally hope to cross the Channel and come to grips with our German enemy under a British commander. His Prime Minister and his Chief of the Imperial Staff are frankly at variance with such a proposal. The shadows of Passchendaele and

[1] See note 1 to p. 35 above.

Dunkerque still hang too heavily over the imagination of these leaders of his government.[1]

So far as the Prime Minister was concerned, this appreciation was not unjust. The enthusiasm for an attack on North-West Europe which he had shown the previous autumn had evaporated. As he was later to confess, 'the fearful price we had to pay in human life and blood for the great offensives of the First World War was graven on my mind. Memories of the Somme and Passchendaele and many lesser frontal attacks upon the Germans were not to be blotted out by time or reflection.'[2] The change in his attitude is significant and not easy to explain. Perhaps it was brought about by the excellence which the Germans had shown as defensive fighters in North Africa. Perhaps his original enthusiasm had been due rather to a desire to conciliate his two powerful allies than to any serious assessment of possibilities. Now that an alternative had presented itself he embraced it with ardour. Flexibility had always been the essence of his strategic thinking. We have seen how he regarded the Mediterranean strategy as providing new opportunities rather than as a fundamental shift of the centre of gravity of the Allied attack, and how he looked forward to pushing 'either right-handed, left-handed or both-handed as our resources and circumstances permit'. To decide now to concentrate on a right-handed push involved no departure from his own strategic concept. That it did involve a unilateral abandonment of an Allied Grand Strategy decided upon only after careful examination of a host of complex and relevant factors and much arduous debate, evidently worried him considerably less than it should.

The position of Sir Alan Brooke, whom Mr Stimson

[1] Henry L. Stimson and McGeorge Bundy, *On Active Service in Peace and War* (New York 1948), p. 436.

[2] Churchill, *The Second World War*, vol. V (London 1952), p. 514.

bracketed with the Prime Minister in his reluctance to launch Operation OVERLORD, is even less easy to justify. At all the great conferences in 1943 – at Casablanca in January, Washington in May, Quebec in August – General Brooke justified the Mediterranean strategy largely in terms of its contribution to the invasion of North-West Europe. It would draw German reserves to the south and keep them there; it would wear down German fighter defences and provide facilities for heavier bombing of Germany; it would provide immediate relief for the hard-pressed Russians. At no point – so far as this writer has been able to discover – did he suggest either to his Allies or to his colleagues on the Chiefs of Staff Committee that the Mediterranean could be a decisive theatre in itself. Yet in his diary for the autumn of 1945 we find two very revealing entries:

[25 October.] Our build-up in Italy is much slower than that of the Germans and far slower than I expected. We shall have to have an almighty row with the Americans who have put us in this position with their insistence to abandon the Mediterranean operations for the very problematical cross-Channel operations. We are now beginning to see the full beauty of the Marshall strategy! It is quite heart-breaking when we see what we might have done this year if our strategy had not been distorted by the Americans. . . .

[1 November.] When I look at the Mediterranean I realise only too well how far I have failed. If only I had had sufficient force of character to swing those American Chiefs of Staff and make them see daylight, how different the war might be. We should have had the whole Balkans ablaze by now, and the war might have finished by 1943.[1]

These comments were neither accurate nor fair. The Americans had at no point 'insisted on abandoning Mediterranean operations'. In the discussion at Quebec in August,

---

[1] Arthur Bryant, *Triumph in the West* (London 1959), pp. 56, 59.

to which General Brooke's entries seem particularly to refer, they had stood firmly by the agreement reached at Washington the previous May, that the forces allotted to General Eisenhower should not be increased and that seven divisions should be returned from his command to the United Kingdom – divisions which were in fact still available to him when the invasion of Italy began. The fact that the agreed Allied Grand Strategy had been entirely successful in achieving its objectives, by bringing about a collapse of the Axis position in the Mediterranean and compelling the German High Command to divert forces from other fronts, did not seem in Washington a valid reason for abandoning it.

Yet by the end of September 1943 there was certainly, in both London and throughout the Mediterranean itself, a bitter sense of opportunities missed, and this was faithfully reflected in General Brooke's unhappy comments. Italy had surrendered. Her forces throughout Yugoslavia, Greece and the Aegean, including the Dodecanese, had abandoned the struggle. But the Allies had little to show for it except a precarious foothold in the Dodecanese – which they were soon humiliatingly to lose – and General Eisenhower's forces grinding to a standstill in the vile campaigning country of Southern Italy. The glittering vistas briefly revealed by the Italian collapse – the Allies overrunning Italy to the Apennines and possibly to the Alps, the links established across the Adriatic with Yugoslav and Greek partisans, the disintegration of the German position in the Balkans and the whole of their south-eastern front, the entry into the war of Turkey, wooed so energetically and so expensively for the past four years, the opening of unrestricted communication with Russia through the Dardanelles – all this vanished as rapidly as a pantomime transformation scene. No wonder the audience was disappointed.

Yet it must again be reiterated that, natural as this dis-

appointment may have been, the Allies had by the end of
1943 achieved all their agreed aims in the Mediterranean.
They had cleared it for shipping – an enormous advantage in
the battle with the U-boats. They had drawn nearly fifty
German divisions into Italy and the Balkan peninsula. They
had captured the airfields around Foggia, and were operating
from them against targets in Central and South-Eastern
Europe with lethal effect. And although they were too late to
save Tito from a rapid German counter-stroke in September,
communications across the Adriatic were opened and strengthened, and within a year the partisans were receiving help
on a massive scale. The appetites which had been disappointed,
especially those for seizing Rhodes and striking across the
Aegean at the mainland of Greece, were largely ones which
had developed *en mangeant* and which had not received
general Allied – or even general Britisn – sanction.

That more was not achieved in the Mediterranean during
the autumn of 1943 was not primarily due to lack of resources,
and certainly not to lack of man-power. What General
Eisenhower needed for the more effective conduct of his
operations was more shipping and above all more landing
craft; and in the allocation of these scarce vessels the Chiefs
of Staff had to take account not only of forthcoming cross-
Channel operations but of Allied commitments, civil as well
as military, all over the world. It is certainly arguable that the
resources available within the Mediterranean could have been
more effectively used. A command system which divided the
area between an Allied Command under General Eisenhower
based on Algiers, with responsibility for the Italian theatre,
and a British Command under General Sir Henry Maitland
Wilson based on Cairo, with responsibility for the Balkan
peninsula and the Aegean, was at best a clumsy mechanism
for rapid and flexible strategic planning under pressure. A
commander with responsibility over the entire Mediterranean

theatre, such as was later created, might have seen Southern Europe as a strategic unit, and made a different allocation of forces for attacking it. Such a commander might have allocated a higher priority to clearing the Aegean and establishing a bridgehead on the Dalmatian coast than he did to the advance on Rome. The latter strategy, involving a campaign in terrain of remarkable difficulty, only pushed the Germans back along their communications and imposed an attrition which worked as effectively on the attacker as on the defence. The former, threatening more directly the German flank in South Russia and her vulnerable resources in the Balkans and bringing more immediate help to the partisan armies, might have imposed a yet greater strain on German resources at lower cost to the Allies; especially since, as hindsight now tells us, the most effective German riposte, the abandonment of the Aegean and the greater part of Greece, was prohibited by Hitler. As it was, Algiers and Cairo found themselves in direct competition for resources, and priorities had to be settled by the Combined Chiefs of Staff.

It is only at this stage of the war that we find the Prime Minister starting to plead for a greater concentration on the Eastern Mediterranean. Operations there, he pointed out to the President on 7 October, would have an impact not only on Greece and Yugoslavia but on Turkey and on Hitler's uneasy and restive satellites, Hungary, Bulgaria and Rumania.

When we remember what brilliant results have followed from the political reactions in Italy induced by our military efforts, should we not be short-sighted to ignore the possibility of a similar and even greater landslide in all the countries I have mentioned? ... I have never wished to send an army into the Balkans, but only by agents, supplies and commandos to stimulate the intense guerrilla [sic] prevailing there. ... What I ask for is the capture of Rhodes and the other islands of the Dodecanese. The movement northward of our Middle East Air Forces and

[50]

their establishment in these islands, and possibly on the Turkish shore, which last might well be obtained, would force a diversion on the enemy far greater than that required of us.[1]

But Mr Churchill did not see these operations as an alternative to the campaign in Italy. Rhodes and Rome both figured in his mind as necessary objectives. As in his interventions in the debate on Allied strategy a year earlier, he wanted to have his cake and eat it, and his military advisers found difficulty in convincing him that this was logistically impossible. Presented with a choice between operations in the Eastern Mediterranean and those in Italy, even the British Chiefs of Staff favoured the former.

As for the Americans, it would not be unfair to say that on this issue they had a closed mind. For them, the scales were weighted by the strong emotions aroused by the very word 'Balkan', with its overtones of European subtlety and intrigue. The area to the east of the Adriatic, in Dr Leighton's words,

... was regarded by American strategists with something akin to the superstitious dread with which medieval mariners once contemplated the unknown monster-infected reaches of the Western Ocean.[2]

Worse, the US Army Planning Staff associated the whole area, somewhat obscurely, with British imperialist designs. As Dr Matloff put it in his official history of *Strategic Planning for Coalition Warfare*:

The indisposition to have United States troops become embroiled in the Balkans was similar to the reluctance to have them take part in the recovery of colonial areas in the Far East. The

[1] John Ehrman, *Grand Strategy*, vol. V (London 1956), p. 95.
[2] Richard M. Leighton, 'Overlord Revisited', *The American Historical Review*, July 1963.

planners felt that on a long-term basis little good and much damage could result from such interference.[1]

In these circumstances it is not surprising that the strategic possibilities of the Eastern Mediterranean received no serious examination at the hands of the Joint Chiefs of Staff. Indeed Dr Matloff himself has written elsewhere: 'It appears clear that back of Churchill's Balkan policy lay the traditional British balance of power theory';[2] a view which has gained very wide acceptance on both sides of the Atlantic.

It is, however, difficult to find any evidence to suggest that in the autumn of 1943 Mr Churchill's policy for the Balkans was inspired by anything more than strategic opportunism. He had recently sent as his personal envoy to Tito, Brigadier Fitzroy Maclean; and when Maclean asked what British policy should be towards Soviet penetration of the Balkans, he received the reply:

So long as the whole of Western civilisation was threatened by the Nazi menace, we could not afford to let our attention be diverted from the immediate issue by considerations of long-term policy. We were as loyal to our Soviet Allies as we hoped they were to us. My task [wrote Maclean] was simply to find out who was killing the most Germans and suggest means by which we could help them to kill more.[3]

As for Eastern Europe, the evidence is strong that not only Churchill but the Foreign Office recognized this as already lying irrevocably within the Soviet sphere of influence. In October, when peace-feelers were received from Rumania, Mr Eden and Mr Cordell Hull, the American Secretary of State, agreed that 'the Soviet Union was entitled to decide

[1] Maurice Matloff, *Strategic Planning for Coalition Warfare 1943–44*, p. 510.
[2] Maurice Matloff, 'The Anvil Decision' in *Command Decisions*, ed. K. R. Greenfield (New York 1959), p. 301.
[3] Fitzroy Maclean, *Eastern Approaches* (London 1950), p. 281.

any such questions concerning Rumania and Hungary and Finland as well – since only its forces were engaged in active warfare against these countries'.[1] The only area in South-East Europe where the British did have the kind of long-term interest which the American planners found so sinister was Greece; and there certainly the Chiefs of Staff had contingency plans for flying in troops, in the event of a German withdrawal, to prevent a take-over of power by the Communist-inspired ELAS bands. In so far as the protection of Greece was associated with the maintenance of Britain's strategic position in the Eastern Mediterranean, these plans can perhaps be cited as examples of British concern for 'interests' of which Washington was suspicious. It is a little ironical that the British decision to abandon those interests some three years later should have caused such consternation in the United States.

There was thus little political motivation in the increasing emphasis which the British placed on Mediterranean operations in the autumn of 1943. But it appeared to the Americans that this emphasis was increasing and that British interest in OVERLORD was correspondingly on the decline. The problems of OVERLORD bulked ever larger as the British examined the German performance in Sicily and Italy – the speed with which the Wehrmacht reacted to emergencies, their capacity for rapid improvisation, the stubbornness and skill with which they fought even when deprived of all air cover. On this point Mr Churchill expressed himself quite frankly in a letter to the President on 23 October:

I do not doubt our ability in the conditions laid down to get ashore and deploy. I am however deeply concerned about the build-up and with the situation which may arise between the thirtieth and the sixtieth days. . . . My dear friend, this is much the

[1] Herbert Feis, *Roosevelt, Churchill and Stalin: the War they Waged and the Peace they Sought* (Princeton 1957), p. 218.

greatest thing we have ever attempted, and I am not satisfied that we have yet taken the measures necessary to give it the best chance of success.[1]

To improve those chances, suggested the British Chiefs of Staff in a memorandum of 11 November, it was desirable to continue with the process of attrition in the Mediterranean:

We must not regard OVERLORD on a fixed date as the pivot of our whole strategy on which all else turns. . . . With the Germans in their present plight . . . we should stretch the German forces to the utmost by threatening as many of their vital interests and areas as possible and, holding them thus, we should attack wherever we can do so in superior force.[2]

The Chiefs of Staff therefore proposed that the Allies should press on in the Mediterranean. They should advance in Italy beyond Rome to the Pisa–Rimini line; they should intensify aid to the partisan armies in the Balkans; they should press Turkey to enter the war and open up the Dardanelles; and they should do 'everything possible to promote a state of chaos and disruption in the satellite Balkan countries'.[3]

The American Joint Chiefs of Staff regarded this programme without enthusiasm. They read into it the clear implication that OVERLORD was once more to be delayed, that still more time would be devoted to indecisive attrition, and that the final decision would be postponed till the Greek kalends. When the matter came up for discussion at the Teheran Conference in November, the Russians made it clear that on this point their sympathies lay emphatically with the Americans. Stalin asked Mr Churchill point-blank whether he believed in OVERLORD at all. The Russian attitude on this question, and the pressure which they brought to bear in

[1] Churchill, *The Second World War*, vol. V, p. 278. *Grand Strategy*, vol. V, pp. 106–7.
[2] *Grand Strategy*, vol. V, p. 111.
[3] Op. cit., p. 111.

favour of OVERLORD and operations directly in support of it, are commonly attributed to their determination to steer the Western Allies away from the Balkans, and there is no doubt considerable justification for this view. But after all the Russians believed in the value of great land battles quite as firmly as did the Americans. They had fought a large number themselves, with increasing skill and success. It is at least conceivable that the American proposals, for a concerted thrust at the centre of German power, should have made sense to them in a way that the small-scale and dispersed operations advocated by the British did not.

Yet the decision ultimately taken at Teheran, at the end of November, was very much in line with the British recommendations. OVERLORD was to be postponed, for not more than a month, to make possible an advance to the Pisa-Rimini line – but on one firm condition: Allied resources in the Mediterranean were then to be used in an operation which would give direct support (or so it was hoped) to OVERLORD – Operation ANVIL, a landing on the southern coast of France. This decision involved no concession by the British Chiefs of Staff, who had an open mind about the course of operations once the Pisa-Rimini line was reached. In their memoranda of this period thrusts westward into southern France or eastward into northern Yugoslavia were discussed as equally acceptable alternatives. Mr Churchill himself accepted the decision with apparent satisfaction. 'The fact that both the Americans and the Russians favoured it,' he afterwards explained, 'made it easier to secure the landing craft necessary for the success of our Italian campaign and the capture of Rome, without which it would have been a failure.'[1] The Combined Chiefs of Staff were therefore able to set their collective hands to an unequivocal statement of intent:

[1] Churchill, *The Second World War*, vol. V, p. 358.

THE MEDITERRANEAN STRATEGY

OVERLORD and ANVIL are the supreme operations for 1944. They must be carried out during May 1944. Nothing must be undertaken in any other part of the world which hazards the success of these two operations.[1]

Neither in his writings at the time nor in his subsequent memoirs did Mr Churchill indicate that he was disturbed at a decision which was likely to involve abandoning much of South-Eastern Europe to the Soviet Union. Indeed he stated quite explicitly in *The Second World War*, 'Surveying the whole military scene, as we separated in an atmosphere of friendship and unity of immediate purpose, I personally was well content'.[2]

Mr Churchill's contentment may seem the more surprising in view of his failure to gain the support of either of his allies for the continuation of the operations in the Eastern Mediterranean which he had been pressing upon them so urgently since the beginning of October. But above even these operations he rated the need to support the armies in Italy, over whose destinies he brooded with such possessive passion.

We must not [he had written to President Roosevelt on 26 October] let this great Italian battle degenerate into a deadlock. *At all costs* we must win Rome and the airfields to the north of it. ... I feel that Eisenhower and Alexander must have what they need to win the battle in Italy, *no matter what effect is produced on subsequent operations* [author's italics].[3]

[1] *Grand Strategy*, vol. V, p. 189.

[2] Churchill, *The Second World War*, vol. V, p. 358. Lord Ismay in his memoirs also wrote of the atmosphere of trust established with the Russians at Teheran (*The Memoirs of Lord Ismay* [London 1960], p. 328). Lord Moran records that immediately after the conference the Prime Minister stated his intention of visiting General Alexander in Italy because 'he may be our last hope. We've got to do something with these bloody Russians.' But he admits that it was only later that it occurred to him to interpret this remark in a hostile sense (Lord Moran, *Churchill* [London 1966], p. 144).

[3] Churchill, *The Second World War*, vol. V, p. 220.

At Teheran he had declared still more publicly that 'he wished it to be placed on record that he could not in any circumstances agree to sacrifice the activities of the armies in the Mediterranean, which included 20 British and British-controlled divisions, merely in order to keep the exact date of 1st May for OVERLORD'.[1] The element of sheer chauvinism, which had been present in Mr Churchill's original arguments for the invasion of Italy, was becoming an ever stronger factor in his strategic thinking as time went on. General Brooke noticed it, and attributed it to the Prime Minister's chagrin at the increasing preponderance of American forces in the European war. 'As a result,' he wrote, 'he became inclined at times to put up strategic proposals which in his heart he knew were unsound, purely to spite the Americans. . . . It was usually fairly easy to swing him back on to the right line. There lay, however, at the back of his mind the desire to form a purely British theatre when the laurels would be all ours.'[2] Certainly there seem to have been moments during the autumn of 1943 when Mr Churchill appeared less interested in the long-term attrition which the Mediterranean strategy might inflict on German forces in Europe than in seeing Generals Alexander and Montgomery riding in triumph through Rome.

Operation ANVIL was thus acceptable to the Prime Minister, as for rather different reasons it was to his Chiefs of Staff, primarily because it made possible the continuation, at full strength, of the Italian campaign.[3] But during the winter of 1943-4 that campaign was to make such slow progress, and

[1] *Grand Strategy*, vol. V, p. 176.

[2] Arthur Bryant, *Triumph in the West*, p. 71.

[3] General Brooke commented after the Teheran Conference: 'I had got the date of OVERLORD pushed on to June 1st so that it would not cripple the Italian campaign, and the South of France offensive turned into something more elastic which can be adjusted without affecting Italy too seriously.' (*Triumph in the West*, p. 109.)

the Germans were to put up so successful a resistance, that by January the proposed landings in the South of France were beginning to figure not as an associate but as a rival operation. If resources were diverted as originally planned, it seemed increasingly doubtful whether the Allied armies would be able to get to Rome at all. General Eisenhower's successor in Algiers, General Sir Henry Maitland Wilson, suggested indeed that ANVIL should be cancelled altogether 'and that I be given a fresh directive to conduct operations with the object of containing the maximum number of German troops in Southern Europe with the forces now earmarked to be placed at my disposal'.[1] The toughness of the fighting in Italy, he argued, was in itself diverting more German forces than anyone had expected. ANVIL therefore was now unnecessary.

The Chiefs of Staff in London accepted this reasoning. The Americans did not. In their eyes it appeared the British were trying once again to wriggle out of a solemn and binding commitment which had itself involved a considerable concession on their own part. They did not accept that operations in Italy could afford the same direct support to OVERLORD as would be a landing in the South of France, and they doubted the wisdom of gambling, as they saw it, on the Germans continuing indefinitely to defend every yard of the Italian peninsula. The option was always open to them of executing a swift, planned withdrawal and switching troops to the north – an operation which Allied forces based on Italy alone would be unable to counter or prevent.

After further discussions the Americans again yielded to the extent of postponing ANVIL until after the capture of Rome. In doing so they threw away half their case. Since the landing would now be delayed until mid-July it would no longer serve its original purpose of facilitating OVERLORD by pinning

[1] *Grand Strategy*, vol. V, p. 231.

down and distracting German reserves at a vital moment. The very title of the operation now made little sense, and it was ultimately changed to the neutral and archaic one of DRAGOON. The intensity of the feelings roused during this controversy can be judged from General Brooke's reaction when the Americans proposed to make available additional landing craft from the Pacific on condition that they were used exclusively for the landings in the South of France. 'History', he wrote in his diary, 'will never forgive them for bargaining equipment against strategy and for trying to blackmail us into agreeing with them by holding the pistol of withdrawing craft at our heads.' History, however, cannot ignore Sir John Dill's description of the Joint Chiefs of Staff as being 'shocked and pained to find out . . . how gaily we proposed to accept their legacy while disregarding the terms of the will'.[1] And History might at this point remind the reader that the whole dispute, bitter as it was, had nothing to do with any conflict between a 'Balkan' and a Western Strategy. The object of the British commanders at this stage – March to April 1944 – was still limited, short-sightedly perhaps, to breaking the German winter line through Cassino, capturing Rome, and pursuing to the Pisa–Rimini line. The possibilities beyond that – a breakthrough into the Po Valley, a landing in the Gulf of Genoa, a landing in Istria, a massive switch of forces to the South of France – still lay in the realm of speculation. They had been barely discussed, let alone decided, by the Chiefs of Staff. General Wilson was simply ordered, in April, to launch an all-out offensive in Italy; to 'develop the greatest possible threat to contain German forces in southern France'; and to 'make plans for the best possible use of the amphibious lift remaining to you, either in support of operations in Italy, or in order to take advantage of

[1] *Triumph in the West*, p. 184. Matloff, *Strategic Planning for Coalition Warfare 1943-44*, pp. 424-5.

opportunities arising in the South of France or elsewhere for the furtherance of your object'.[1]

It thus appears that, although the Chiefs of Staff were still doubtful whether the South of France landings should take place at all, they had at this stage no clear alternative to put forward in their place. The Americans had no such doubts. Rome fell on 4 June; the OVERLORD landings took place on 6 June; and the last great controversy over 'the Mediterranean Strategy' began.

The Americans pressed for the South of France landings to take place as and when they had been agreed. Their arguments were now based on considerations of logistics rather than of strategy: only if Toulon and Marseilles were in their possession, they maintained, could they build up their forces rapidly enough to overwhelm the German defences and strike quickly at the heart of the enemy. The argument seemed reasonable enough at a time when the Allied forces in North-West Europe were being supplied over beaches through a single artificial harbour, the second having been broken up by storms. General Eisenhower, now Supreme Allied Commander of the forces invading North-West Europe, predictably supported the stand of the Joint Chiefs of Staff, and he did so in terms which once more stated the basic US Army philosophy. 'France,' he wrote, 'is the decisive theatre. The Combined Chiefs of Staff took this decision long ago. In my view the resources of Great Britain and the United States will *not* allow us to maintain two major theatres in the European War, each with decisive missions.'[2] It could convincingly be maintained that the Mediterranean theatre had fulfilled the strategic function allotted to it by every Allied Conference since Casablanca, of imposing a heavy strain on the German forces and making possible the landings

[1] *Grand Strategy*, vol. V, p. 259.
[2] Ibid., p. 349.

in North-West Europe at acceptable cost, and that now it could be run down. The preparatory phase was over: the decisive battle must now begin.

This view was later accepted even by that champion of the Mediterranean strategy, General Brooke.

Now at last [he wrote as a gloss on his diary entry of 11 June 1944] we had put the South of France operation in its right strategic position. By the time we had reached the Pisa–Rimini line the Italian theatre should have played its part in holding German reserves away from Northern France. We could then contemplate the landing in Southern France to provide a front for French forces from North Africa and to co-operate on the southern flank of OVERLORD operations.[1]

At the time, however, he was not prepared to adopt so philosophic an attitude. It quickly became known in London that Hitler had forbidden a precipitate withdrawal to the Pisa–Rimini line and had ordered his forces in Italy, once again, to contest every yard of the ground. The battle in Italy was by no means over, and the Chiefs of Staff objected to depriving General Alexander of any significant part of his forces until he had won it. Their arguments, that he was effectively pinning down German forces in Italy, were now, however, irrelevant to the American contention that they needed the French Mediterranean ports for their logistical build-up. Not surprisingly, they were received in Washington with no sympathy at all.

It does not appear that even at this stage the British Chiefs of Staff had any clear programme for the further development of the Italian front, beyond drawing more German forces into the area and destroying them. But General Alexander, understandably elated by his victory, was developing a more ambitious programme. On 7 June, three days after the fall of Rome, he reported the morale of his troops to be

[1] Arthur Bryant, *Triumph in the West*, p. 211.

'irresistibly high. . . . Neither the Apennines nor even the Alps should prove a serious obstacle to their enthusiasm and skill'.[1] If he were left his full force of twenty-seven divisions, he claimed, he would be able to break through the Apennines to the Po valley, reach the river Piave north of Venice with eighteen divisions, and carry the 'Ljubljana Gap', through which the main road and railway ran from Italy into northern Yugoslavia.

Once through the so-called Ljubljana Gap [wrote Lord Alexander in his memoirs] the way led to Vienna, an object of great political and psychological value. . . . The terrain between Trieste and the Drava river is mountainous, but not more so than much of Italy over which we had advanced successfully; and troops which could overcome a brave and stubborn enemy such as we had met in the Apennine ranges north of Florence would surely not be stopped by what we might find in Yugoslavia and beyond.[2]

This sanguine view, which was widely shared at General Alexander's headquarters,[3] awoke no echo whatever in Washington. It was sceptically received even by the British Chiefs of Staff. President Roosevelt, refusing to abandon the South of France landings in favour of such an operation, suggested tactfully that General Alexander, 'for several natural and very human reasons' was underestimating the difficulties that lay ahead of him. General Brooke pointed out to the Prime Minister 'that even on Alex's optimistic reckoning, the advance beyond the Pisa–Rimini line would not start

---

[1] *Grand Strategy*, vol. V, p. 267.

[2] Field Marshal Earl Alexander of Tunis, *The Alexander Memoirs 1940–45* (London 1962), p. 138.

[3] See e.g. Marshal of the R.A.F. Sir John Slessor, *The Central Blue* (London 1957), p. 588. 'As a matter of fact this was a very unduly optimistic appreciation, though I did not think so at the time – everyone in Italy was still too cock-a-hoop at the capture of Rome and no one foresaw the skilful and dogged defence that we had still to overcome.'

till after September; namely, we should embark on a campaign through the Alps in the winter . . . if we took the season
of the year and the topography of the country in league
against us, we should have three enemies instead of one'.[1] But
in Mr Churchill General Alexander found an enthusiastic
supporter. Not only did the Prime Minister long to see what
he described as 'the most representative Army of the British
Empire now in the field' end up in a blaze of glory.[2] He was
now, for the first time, beginning to worry about the spread
of Russian influence in Eastern Europe.

We have observed the equanimity with which, in autumn
1943, Mr Churchill had contemplated Russian dominance in
the Balkans. In December Brigadier Maclean, fresh from his
mission to the Yugoslav partisans, had reported to him that
Tito would certainly swing Yugoslavia strongly towards the
Soviet Union. 'Do you intend,' asked the Prime Minister in
reply, 'to make Yugoslavia your home after the war? . . .
Neither do I. And that being so, the less you and I worry
about the form of Government they set up, the better. That
is for them to decide. What interests us is, which of them is
doing the most harm to the Germans.'[3] In May 1944 he
sponsored a proposal to leave the Russians a leading rôle in
Rumania (to which he later added Bulgaria) in return for
non-interference with British influence in Greece.[4] The
Foreign Office appears to have acquiesced in this division of
the spoils. On 2 May, in a discussion among the War Cabinet
about the bombing of French civilians, Mr Eden voiced his
disquiet at the possibility of antagonizing these friendly
elements since 'After the war, Eastern Europe and the

[1] *Triumph in the West*, p. 223.

[2] *Grand Strategy*, vol. V, p. 393.

[3] Fitzroy Maclean, *Eastern Approaches*, p. 402.

[4] Churchill, *The Second World War*, vol. VI (London 1954), p. 65. E. L.
Woodward, *British Foreign Policy in the Second World War* (London 1962),
p. 292.

Balkans would be largely dominated by Russia, whereas the peoples of Western Europe would look to us.'[1] In October Mr. Churchill was to visit Moscow and conclude the business-like division of power with Stalin which yielded 90 per cent control of Rumania and 75 per cent of Bulgaria to the Soviet Union in return for Britain retaining 90 per cent control in Greece and Yugoslavia being shared on a 50-50 basis. So long as Greece could be kept within the Western sphere of influence, the British government was prepared to acquiesce in Russian dominance of the territories which lay to the north.

But during the summer there can be no doubt of the Prime Minister's alarm at the approach of the Russian armies. Lord Moran, his personal physician and inseparable companion, noted how during August 'Winston never talks of Hitler these days; he is always harping on the dangers of Communism. He dreams of the Red Army spreading like a cancer from one country to another. It has become an obsession, and he seems to think of little else.'[2] In London alarm at Russian intentions and methods as their armies entered Eastern Europe had been growing for some months past. On 7 June the Foreign Office had circulated a paper to the War Cabinet which described the manner in which the Russians were using communist-led movements to gain positions of dominance in South-East Europe, and Mr Eden had observed: 'There are unhappily increasing signs of Russia's intention to play her own hand in the Balkans regardless of our desires and interests, e.g. in Greece.'[3] Over the future government of Poland friction was of still longer standing. The previous February Mr Eden had confessed that the Russian attitude

---

[1] Tedder, *With Prejudice* (London 1966), p. 529.

[2] Lord Moran, *Winston Churchill: The Struggle for Survival* (London 1966), p. 173.

[3] Avon, *The Reckoning*, p. 459.

over the question raised 'most disquieting thoughts' whether Russia would ever co-operate with the West.[1] In August the approach of the Red Army triggered off the tragic and premature rising of the freedom fighters in Warsaw. Not only did the Russians refuse all help to the Polish insurgents; they refused also landing and refuelling facilities to the Allied bombers from Italy which were prepared, at great risk, to fly over and drop supplies. 'The outbreak in Warsaw,' alleged the Russian authorities, 'is purely the work of adventurers and the Soviet government cannot lend its hand to it.' When in September they changed their minds, it was too late. 'As the European war entered on its last phase,' in Mr Ehrman's sombre words, 'the shadow of Warsaw lay over British strategic thought.' Air Marshal Sir John Slessor, the officer responsible for organizing the airdrops, expressed the feelings of many of his countrymen at the time in less restrained terms: 'How, after the fall of Warsaw, any responsible statesman could trust any Russian Communist further than he could kick him, passes the comprehension of ordinary men.'[2]

Yet by August the decision to divert forces from Italy to DRAGOON had already been taken. Mr Roosevelt had given his final decision on 2 July. The decision may subsequently have been regretted on both sides of the Atlantic, but at no stage in the very thorough discussions which had preceded it had the desirability of forestalling the Russians in Central Europe been cited as an argument in favour of General Alexander's plans. Nor were any serious calculations produced to show that these plans were feasible, and it may be doubted whether any were ever made. The evidence of General Alexander himself does not suggest that they were.

It was a dazzling idea, this grand project of reaching Vienna

[1] Woodward, op. cit., p. 285.
[2] *Grand Strategy*, vol. V, p. 376. Slessor, *The Central Blue*, p. 612.

before our Russian allies, and we discussed it informally at my headquarters. Yet it would have been premature to start planning such an operation before it was certain that we could reach the valley of the Po before the end of 1944.[1]

The difficulties would have been considerable. An army advancing north-east beyond Venice would have had first to force a succession of river lines between the Piave and the Isonzo, and carry the formidable positions beyond, which the Austrians had successfully held against repeated Italian attacks during the First World War. An amphibious operation might have done something to reduce the difficulties of this task, but the precedent of Anzio was not an entirely happy one. The 'Ljubljana Gap' which would then confront it is a col some 2,000 feet high and thirty miles wide, with complete command over the slopes up which the Allies would have had to approach. The Gap then leads only to the valley of the Save. To reach Vienna from that valley it would have been necessary first to cross the Karawanken mountains, a range whose peaks rise to 6,000 feet and through which run only two twisting mountain roads, to descend into the Klagenfurt valley. From there the roads run to Vienna, 200 miles beyond, through valleys which frequently narrow to provide easily defensible positions. The powers of recovery of the German forces were a matter of record. They would be falling back along their own lines of communication; at the Ljubljana Gap they would have had a front to defend about one-quarter of the length of the Pisa–Rimini line; and as they withdrew into the Alps they could have moved reinforcements with increasing ease from other fronts. Finally, the distance from Rome to Vienna is some 600 miles – about three times the distance from Naples to Rome which it had taken the Allies six months to cover. In view of all this, Lord Alexander's assurance, that 'troops which could over-

[1] *The Alexander Memoirs*, p. 138.

come a brave and stubborn enemy such as we had met in the Apennine ranges north of Florence would surely not be stopped by what we might find in Yugoslavia or beyond', needs more detailed substantiation to sound at all convincing. General Brooke, as we have seen, was not convinced.

Alex's talk about his advance [he wrote to General Wilson early in August] killed all our arguments stone dead. It is a pity, because I do not see Alex advancing on Vienna this year unless he does it in the face of a crumbling Germany, and in that case he has ample forces for the task and greater than he will be able to administer over snow-covered passes.[1]

The alternative to ANVIL–DRAGOON which the British Chiefs of Staff were urging on their American colleagues was thus *not* an operation to forestall the Russians in Vienna or the Balkans. It was a continuation of the battle of attrition in Italy. They desired, they told the Joint Chiefs of Staff on 26 June, that General Alexander should be allowed to 'continue to develop the full power of his offensive in Italy with the object of engaging and destroying all German armies opposed to him'.[2] Even if such a battle had led to the total collapse of the German forces in Italy, a pursuit to Vienna through terrain where even comparatively small units could have imposed repeated delays, would have been a very difficult matter indeed. And with the Russian armies already spreading over Rumania, Bulgaria and Hungary, with Yugoslavia already liberated by communist-led partisans who regarded the Allied armies with much suspicion and some dislike, it is hard to see how such an operation, even if successful, could have affected the post-war balance in South-Eastern Europe which the Western allies had already virtually accepted at Teheran. It is thus difficult to agree at any point with the judgement of General Mark Clark, who com-

[1] *Triumph in the West*, p. 256.
[2] *Grand Strategy*, vol. V, p. 351.

manded the Allied ground forces under General Alexander, when he asserts that 'the weakening of the campaign in Italy in order to invade Southern France instead of pushing on into the Balkans, was one of the outstanding political mistakes of the war'.[1]

Mark W. Clark, *Calculated Risk* (London 1951), p. 348.

# Conclusion

IT has been argued in the above pages that the British did not present their Allies with a coherent 'Mediterranean Strategy' based either on their historical experience or on their prophetic insights into the problems of the post-war world. Certainly they did not oppose any such strategic concept to the American proposal for a concentration on North-West Europe. In the propositions which the British Chiefs of Staff presented at the Washington Conference in December 1941, the Mediterranean figured as a major theatre because Britain had a position to defend there and resources which could be put to immediate effect against the enemy. When the Americans proposed that this initial period of 'closing the ring' should be followed by a concentrated thrust in North-West Europe in 1943, the British were able to agree without any change in their own long-term plans. The ROUND-UP plan was to be abandoned, not as a result of any British pressure, but because President Roosevelt insisted that United States forces must be in action against the Germans in 1942, and because an operation in French North Africa was the only one which, either at the time or in retrospect, seemed to make strategic sense. It was only after this decision had been taken that the British Chiefs of Staff began to urge the advantages of continuing operations in the Mediterranean; and they did so to counter the arguments, not of those who wished to return to the ROUND-UP concept at the earliest opportunity, but of those in Washington who wanted to revise America's basic strategic priorities and abandon the whole principle of 'Europe First'. Throughout 1943 Medi-

F

terranean operations were justified as necessary preliminaries for the attack on North-West Europe which, all were agreed, was to follow the following summer. They were seen neither as an easy way into Europe (in spite of Mr Churchill's unfortunate 'underbelly' metaphor), nor as a way of forestalling the Russians. The desire to bring to the Soviet Union immediate and continuing help by drawing Axis forces to the South was one of the principal arguments used to justify not only the original landing in North Africa but the invasion of Sicily and the fighting in Italy itself. Even in Mr Churchill's thinking the idea of a forestalling operation appears only briefly during a few exceptional weeks in the summer of 1944 – and then in support of an operation the practicability of which was not self-evident and which was flatly rejected by his own Chiefs of Staff.

Yet towards the end of 1943 one can detect a shift of ground on the part of the British war leaders. Increasingly they appear to have abandoned their own earlier arguments and to have regarded the Mediterranean theatre, not as subsidiary, but as an end in itself, the success of whose operations was its own justification. Mr Churchill's views were tinged by a streak of nationalism which his countrymen can find endearing without expecting anyone else to agree. As for the Chiefs of Staff, their determination not to commit forces to action in North-West Europe until everything possible had been done to weaken an opponent who seemed no less formidable for his performance in Italy showed a proper professional concern which was, however, open to uncharitable interpretations. At this stage it was necessary for the Americans to use all their strength to hold the British to the agreed strategy, and ensure that operations designed as subsidiary should remain so. The United States had cause to be grateful to British caution and realism during the early years of strategic planning; but it was thanks largely to the stubborn perseverance of the American military leaders that that strategy, for better or worse, was ultimately carried out as had been jointly planned. An effective case has still to be made out, that there could have been any more rapid or economical way of winning the war.

# Index

Adriatic Sea, 43, 48–9, 51
Aegean Islands, 10, 35, 41–3, 48–50
Aegean Sea, 49–50
Africa, *see* North Africa, etc.
Aircraft, 13, 26
Aircraft carriers, 4
Air Force, *see* Royal Air Force, etc.
Air power, 4, 7, 26
Alanbrooke, Lord, *see* Brooke, General Sir Alan
Alexander, General Sir Harold, 37, 39, 56 and n. 2, 57, 61–3, 65–7
Algeria, 31, 33
Algiers, 39–40, 49–50, 58
Alps, 48, 62–3, 66
Ambrosio, General, 41
America, *see* United States of America
Amphibious warfare, 3–4, 16, 26, 66
'Anaconda' strategy, 17
ANVIL Operation, 55–7, and n. 3, 58–62, 65, 67
Anzio, 66
Apennines, 43, 48, 62, 66–7
Armoured warfare, 6–7, 13–14
Army, *see* separately British Army, Red Army, etc.
Atlantic Ocean, 21, 28–9, 33, 36, 52, 65. *See also* Battle of Atlantic
Auchinleck, General Sir Claud, 16
Australia, 10, 21
Austria, 66–7
AVALANCHE Operation, 44–5
AXIS Operation, 41–3

Balkans, Allied diplomacy in, 6, 10–11, 24; German campaign in, 7; Sub-

version in, 8, 39, 47, 50, 54; German supplies from 8–9, 42, 50; possible reaction in, to Italian defeat, 10, 42, 48; German interests in, 11; proposed Balkan League, 11; plans for Allied entry into, 18, 20, 43; US suspicions of British interests in, 24, 51; German commitments in, following Italian collapse, 35, 42–3, 48–9; possible Allied landings in, 37, 43, 47–8, 50, 52; Allied aid to, 39, 48, 50, 54; Italian hold on slackens, 39, 41, 48; Middle East HQ responsible for, 49; PM's suggested strategy for, 50–2; possible Soviet penetration of, 52; in Soviet sphere of interest, 52–3, 55–6, 63–4; Churchill/Stalin deal on interests in, 64; possible forestalling of Russia in, 67–8
Battle of the Atlantic, 8, 21, 28
Bauxite, 42
Belgium, 3, 23
Bengal, Bay of, 27
Blockade, 6, 8, 12–14, 16–17, 19
BOLERO Operation, 26, 29, 32
Bombing offensive, 6, 9, 12–14, 16, 19, 22, 35, 39, 43, 47, 51, 63–4
Brest, 29
British Army, traditional strategy of, 1–2, 7; return of, to Continent, 7–9, 13–15, 26; estimated strength of, 8–9, 26; deployment of, 9, 22, 26, 39; in Middle East, 9–10, 36; withdrawal of, from Greece and Crete, 11, 23; pre-war training of,

gives SOE directive, 12; at First Washington Conference, 13–14, 18, 24; strategic memorandum of, December 1941, 13–15, 18; US Forces, doubts about, 23; views of, on US proposals for N.W. Europe, 27, 29, 45–6; accepts US plans for N.W. Europe, 27; visits Washington, 29, 31; raises Operation GYMNAST with President, 31–3; views of, on Mediterranean strategy, 31, 39–40, 44–6, 50–1, 56–7, 70; refuses to believe in postponement of ROUND-UP, 32; intervenes with President on TORCH landings, 33; divergence of views from COS on Mediterranean strategy, 34–5; informs Stalin on Mediterranean strategy, 34; enthusiasm of, for Italian campaign, 39, 44–5, 55–7; at Trident Conference, 39; visits North Africa, 39; writes to Smuts, 39–40; suggests South of France landings, 45, 57; Stimson reports on views of, to President, 45–7; doubts of, on OVERLORD, 46, 53–4, 57; flexibility of strategic thought of, 46; presses for Eastern Mediterranean strategy, 50–1, 56–7; sends envoy to Tito, 52, 63; conversations of, with Stalin at Teheran, 54–6; accepts Soviet influence in S.E. Europe, 56, 63; visits Italy, 56 n. 2; Chauvinism of, 57, 63, 70; views of, on Alexander's plan to cross the Alps, 62–5, 70; starts worrying about Soviet influence in Eastern Europe, 63, 70; agreement with Stalin on spheres of interest, 64

Clark, General Mark, 67–8
Clausewitz, Karl Marie von, 5
Combined Chiefs of Staff, cumbrous

machinery of, 26; views of, on operations in North Africa, 29; views of, on 'Tightening the Ring', 31; views of, on Mediterranean strategy, 36; at Casablanca, 36; at Washington (TRIDENT), 36–7; settle priorities in the Mediterranean, 50; Eastern Mediterranean strategy not seriously considered by, 52; Teheran decisions of, 55–6; OVERLORD decisions of, 60

Combined Operations HQ, 30
Communism, 64
Conferences, at Placentia, August 1941, 13, 21; at Washington, December 1941, 13–14, 16–20, 22, 24, 31, 69; at Teheran, November 1943, 23, 54–6, and n. 3, 67; in London, 1942, 27–9; at Casablanca, January 1943, 35–6, 45–6, 60; at Washington (TRIDENT) May 1943, 36–9, 45–7; at Quebec, August 1943, 47–8
Copper, 42
Corsica, 35, 38
Crete, 11
Cross-Channel Concept, see OVERLORD
CRUSADER Operation, 16, 31

Dalmatia, see Yugoslavia
Dalton, Dr Hugh, 12
Dardanelles, 31, 48, 54
Defence Committee, 27
Dieppe, 30
Dill, Field Marshal Sir John, 11, 25, 59
Dodecanese Islands, 37, 43, 48, 50
Dönitz, Admiral, 43
DRAGOON Operation, see ANVIL
Drava River, 62
Dunkirk, 46

Eastern Front, 16, 35, 42

Great Britain—*cont.*

strategic problems of, after French defeat, 7–10; German blockade of, 8; resources of, 9; Command of the Seas of, 9; sources of oil for, 9; Greek interests of, 10–12, 53, 63–4; official strategic doctrine of, 14–15, 22, 29; security of, 19, 24; US resources for, 22, 26, 33; mobilization of, 22, 26; American reluctance to defend 'British interests', 24–5, 51–3; US forces in, 26, 29, 32; veto of, on SLEDGEHAMMER, 30; plans of, for defeat of Japan, 33; reported weakening of determination of, for OVERLORD, 45; forces returned from the Mediterranean to, 48; unable to support two major European theatres, 60; influence of, in Yugoslavia, 64; alarm in, of Russian intentions, 64–5; subsequent regrets in, over ANVIL, 65, 69; Mediterranean interests of, 69

Greece, British landings in, 4, 11, 23, 43, 45, 48–50, 53; British interests in, 10–12, 53, 63–4; Italian invasion of, 11; proposed Balkan League, 11; German invasion of, 11; Government in exile of, 11; resistance in, 11, 54; German forces in, 42–3, 50, 53; collapse of Italian forces in, 48

GYMNAST Operation, *see* TORCH

Hitler, Adolf, hold on Europe, 4, 17; advised on importance of Middle East, 12; failure of Russian plans of, 15; Duce visits at Feltre, 41; fears of, for Balkan supplies, 42; views of, on Italian surrender, 42–3; moves forces to Mediterranean, 42–4; advised to shorten Mediterranean lines, 42–3, 50; decides to fight in Southern Italy, 43–4; forbids with-

drawal to Pisa-Rimini line, 61; PM ceases to worry about, 64

Holland, 3

Hull, Cordell, 52–3

Hungary, 50, 53, 67

HUSKY Operation, *see* Sicily

Iberian Peninsula, 3, 15

India, 10, 22

Indian Ocean, 26

Iraq, 9

Ireland, 13

Ismay, General Lord, 56 n. 2

Isonzo River, 66

Istria, 59

Italy, belligerency of, 9–10; results of defeat of, 10, 43, 48; plans for offensive against, 17, 35, 37–8, 40–1; British views on invasion of, 35, 37–9; defeat of forces of, in North Africa, 37, 39, 41; collapse of, 37, 41–4, 48; hold of, on Balkans, slackens, 39, 41, 48; plans for landing in Southern, 39–40, 48; PM's enthusiasm for campaign in, 39, 44–5, 55–7; Allied air bases in, 39, 43, 49, 56, 65; forces of, in Sicily, 41, 44; army revolt against Mussolini, 41; overthrow of Mussolini, 41–2; German forces in, 42–3, 47, 49–50, 57–61, 67, 70; surrender of, 42, 48; Allied forces in, 42, 47–8, 50, 56–7, 61–3, 65, 70; slowness of Allied advance in, 43, 48, 50, 57–8, 60–1, 70; Allied plans for further operations in, 44–5, 50–1, 54–7 and n. 3, 58–61, 67, 70; Eisenhower responsible for, 49, 56; PM visits, 56 n. 2; Hitler orders prolonged defence of, 61; Alexander's plans for crossing Alps from, 61–3, 65–7; plans to fly help from, to Poland, 65; forces from, diverted to ANVIL,

65, 67–8; attack on Austria from, 66

Japan, 9, 20, 27–8, 33
Jodl, General, 42–3
Joint Chiefs of Staff, *see* US Joint Chiefs of Staff
Joint Planning Staff, 1941 appreciations of, 12–13; appreciation of, for Washington Conference, 16; views of, on Cross-Channel operations, 28; views of, on SLEDGEHAMMER, 29–30; views on 'follow-up' for TORCH, 34–5; views of, on invasion of Italy, 35, 37–9, 42; views on Mediterranean strategy, 37, 42; PM instructs, on Italian campaign, 44
Joint Staff Mission, 28

Karawanken Mountains, 66
Kesselring, General, 43
Klagenfurt, 66

Landing craft, 4, 49, 59
Lebanon, 10
Leighton, Dr Richard M., 51
Libya, 16
Liddell-Hart, Col. B. H., 6–7
Lincoln, Abraham, 17
Lisbon, 41
Ljubljana Gap, 62, 66
London, 11, 16, 27, 29, 45, 48, 61, 64

Maclean, Brigadier Fitzroy, 52, 63
Madrid, 10
Maitland-Wilson, General Sir Henry, 49, 58–60, 67
Malta, 16
Manpower, 49
Marseilles, 60
Marshall, General, lack of amphibious

experience of, 23; friendship of, with Dill, 23; approves plans for invasion of N.W. Europe, 26–9; London talks of, 26–9; views of, on TORCH, 32–3; determination of, that OVERLORD take precedence over Mediterranean, 37–8, 44; views of, on Italian campaign, 40, 44–5, 47; visits Algiers with PM, 40; proposes Allied landing at Naples, 44; strategy of, criticized by Brooke, 47
Matloff, Dr Maurice, 51–2
Mediterranean Sea, role of Royal Navy in, 9; Spanish threat to, 10; British interests in Eastern, 11; plans for reopening to Allied shipping, 16–17, 33, 37, 49; plans for return to Europe across, 18, 20; reopening of, 37, 49; threat to Axis defences in Western, 38; French ports in, needed for Allied build-up, 60–1
Mediterranean Theatre, possible diversion of German troops to, 12, 49, 54, 69–70; planning for operations in, 16, 28–9, 31, 35; US resources for, 21, 32–3, 49; US suspicion of operations in, 24, 32, 53; Churchill's strategic views on, 31, 44–6, 70; differences between British and US staffs on landings in, 33, 60; differences between PM and COS on strategy in, 34; liability for Germany of, 35–6, 42–6, 48, 60, 69–70; aspects of strategy in, 36–7, 46, 48–9, 53–6, 60, 69–71; diversion of forces to, 37–8; withdrawal of forces from, 38, 48–9; Allied forces in, 39–40, 69; Brooke's views on strategy in, 47–8, 61; Allied aims achieved in, 49, 60–1, 70; Allied resources and manpower in, 49–50; lack of shipping for, 49; command

# INDEX

Shipping—*cont.*
OVERLORD in 1943, 36; shortage of, in Mediterranean, 49
Sicily, British desire to control Straits of, 33; invasion of (HUSKY) agreed, 35, 37–41, 44–5, 70; Italian forces in, 41, 44; German forces in, 43
SLEDGEHAMMER Operation, 26, 29–30
Slessor, Marshal of the R.A.F., Sir John, 62 n. 3, 65
Smuts, Field Marshal, 39–40
SOE, *see* Special Operations Executive
Solomon Islands, 32
Somme, 23, 46
South Africa, 10
Soviet Union, *see* Russia
Spain, 10, 33
Special Operations Executive, 12–13
Stalin, Marshal, 34, 54–6, and n. 2, 64
Stimson, Henry L., 45–7
*Strategic Planning for Coalition Warfare*, 51
Subversion, *see also* Patriot Forces, Special Operations Executive, etc., 8, 12–13, 19
Suez Canal, 10
Syria, 10

Teheran, *see* Conferences
Third Reich, *see* Germany
Thrace, 43
Tito, Marshal, 49–50, 63
TORCH Operation, 29, 31–3
Toulon, 60
Trident Conference, *see* Conferences
Trieste, 62
Tripoli, 16
Turkey, British influence in, 9; Balkan League, 11; British diplomatic action in, 11–12; plans for Allied entry into the Balkans from,

18, 20; place in Allied strategic planning, 18, 20, 37, 50; Allied attempts to get into the war, 37, 50, 54; possible Allied air bases in, 50–1

U-boats, 19, 28, 49
United Kingdom, *see* Great Britain
United Nations, 36
United States of America, lack of strategic experience of, 1, 22–3; resources of, 9, 21–2; no military help from, in 1941, 12; entry into the war of, 15, 20–1; historical strategy in, 17; security of, 19; strategy of 'Germany First' accepted by, 20, 29, 69; plans of, for defeat of Japan, 20, 69; allocation of resources by, 21–2, 26, 32–3; reluctance of, to defend 'British interests', 24–5, 51–2; moves to engage American public opinion in Europe, 31; Consular Representatives of, in North Africa, 31; postwar views of, on British influence in Eastern Mediterranean, 53; belief in large land-campaigns, 55; unable to support two major European theatres, 60; subsequent regrets in, over ANVIL, 65
US Army, plans for European landings by, 14–15, 32; lack of understanding between US Navy and, 20; expansion programme of, 21; move of, to UK, 29–32; President's determination to get into battle in 1942, 30–1, 36, 69; reluctance of Joint Chiefs to commit to TORCH, 33; in North Africa, 36; use of, in Mediterranean, 39; views of, on Italian campaign, 40; Stimson Secretary of, 45
US Army Planning Staff, 21, 24–5, 51–3

[82]